Man
Detox

VERITY GEERE

Man Detox

MY FUNNY, SEXY, HEARTBREAKING ADVENTURES IN THE WORLD OF DIGITAL DATING

SO HO FRIDAY

Soho Friday Media Ltd.,
3-4 Temple Bar Business Park,
Strettington Lane, Goodwood,
Chichester, West Sussex,
PO18 OTU

www.sohofriday.com

www.facebook.com/soho.Friday
twitter.com/@sohofriday
www.instagram.com/sohofriday/

First published in paperback in 2019

1 3 5 7 9 10 8 6 4 2

British Library Cataloguing-in-Publication Data:

A catalogue record for this book is available from the British Library.

ISBN: 978 1 91309 406 5

Printed and bound by CPI Group (UK) Ltd, Croydon CR0 4YY

Papers used by Soho Friday Media Ltd. are natural, recyclable products made
from wood grown in sustainable forests. The manufacturing processes conform
to the environmental regulations of the country of origin.

Every reasonable effort has been made to trace copyright-holders of
material reproduced in this book, but if any have been inadvertently overlooked
the publishers would be glad to hear from them.

Disclaimer
**This book started off as a blog, under a pseudonym, but resulted in this
book in my real name. All names and identifying details have been changed
to protect the identity of individuals. The views, thoughts and opinions
expressed in the book are my own.**

Contents

Acknowledgements

Thank you to all of my beautiful friends and family
who supported me to spill my heart in this book.
You know who you are!

Chapter 1

NOmenBER

It's 31 October and I feel like I have reached the depths of dating depravity. After twenty-five years of dating and relationships I have still not found what I'm looking for. I'm so desperate to get out of this cycle, I've got to do something different. So, for the first time in my life, I'm not going to look.

My name is Verity Geere and in some respects I feel like one of the luckiest people alive. I have a stable job, which I love, working as a radio presenter and newsreader. I have lived all over the world, met incredible people and have amazing friends and family, and enjoy a lot of the benefits of being a single woman in her late thirties.

I also feel like I've enjoyed all of the 'joys' of a dating revolution. However, I also feel like a victim of the digital dating age. By this I mean, I remember early dating in my teens before mobiles. When I was passed a note in class at school, or waited by the house phone in the hallway for boys to call and arrange a date. Followed by the advent of pagers, when you would get a digital message on a clunky, plastic thing strapped to your wrist which buzzed and spelt out the interaction/instruction, 'Hi, call me, thanks'.

This was shortly followed by the explosion of mobile phones, when it started as a novelty to send texts and call each other. But then it quickly became the norm to play out huge parts of a relationship over this little brick called a 'mobile' that we suddenly couldn't live without. The problem is, I think a lot of the time people say things in the digital world they wouldn't say in person, which can sometimes completely skew the course of a relationship. The old-school mobiles were soon eclipsed by smart phones, followed by the ability to use mobile phone apps for online dating.

Who knew, when I was born in 1979 and my parents looked down at baby Verity, that this is what my life would come to – the quick, yet soulless act of swiping right ('Yes') or left ('No') on a man's face on dating apps. This was designed to meet Mr Right but instead led to a bunch who have been either Mr All-Right, Mr Right-Now or Mr No-Chance.

I have met many men in real life through friends, work and socialising, but I have also met men through the plentiful and frivolous world of swiping right. I went through a phase in my early thirties, when I attended at least seven weddings a year. Half or more of all those couples met online, proving it can be a highly successful method of matchmaking. But so many of those relationships were the lucky ones, who hit it off with someone within the first few dates.

Bloody Maria, for example, met her husband Guy on her *first* online match. They went out for dinner, cinema, drinks and walks, discovered they had lots in common, fancied each other and became boyfriend and girlfriend. A year later they moved in together, got engaged soon after, followed by the fairytale wedding in a country house and a year later the first baby came along. Textbook! If Ikea sold flatpack relationships, theirs would be it – perfectly acceptable, nice, safe, few screws along the way, straightforward and lasts a lifetime. Why can't all online relationships be as easy as a Billy bookcase?

If you are compatible and you both want to have sex immediately when you meet, why not? Bloody Maria was more patient and ladylike – she made Guy wait several weeks before doing the deed. Is this the key to a long-lasting relationship or does it really matter if you sleep with someone on a first date? However, when it comes to online dating are too many girls making it too easy for men, which is why they don't commit? If you get the milk for free, why would you milk the cow (or whatever the saying is!). But if men don't get their end away, do they still disappear without a trace?

On a number of occasions, I've gone on a first date repeating to myself 'Don't go home with them' and then one thing leads to another and *bang* (quite literally). When it comes to women like Bloody Maria, maybe she caught online dating at the right time. Just before the advent of dating apps, whereby it became 'acceptable' to treat people like a game. I think so many men (and women) enter the magical sweet-shop of online dating and get greedy. Who can blame them? You can have whatever you want: a blonde woman one minute, brunette the next, black woman another night, ginger one the next, thin one, followed by a plus-sized model the next, etc.

Basically, online dating can be like playing the '80s board game Guess Who? Ticking off Sarah, Anita, Anne, Clare etc. It can also be like an addictive game of Snap: inanely passing the time, swiping right and getting a match. If you have never done it before, getting a match can give you quite a high. But after a short while, the adrenaline rush fades and instead just gives you a repetitive strain injury in your wrist, like too much wanking. The constant plethora of dates available also encourages and almost celebrates multi-dating. For me this fertilises a culture of insecurity, whereby you never know whether you are a potential girlfriend or just Miss Tuesday ... Wednesday ... or Friday.

I have friends who swipe right on everyone, so they are constantly 'winning' at Snap and always have a date lined up or someone to chat to. Don't get me wrong: I have met some great people, but I have also met many men with the morals of an alley cat. Some supposed rough diamonds who turned out to be just rough. And some men I would never normally have come into contact with in my normal path of life. I genuinely believe that you meet your type of person depending on where you work, where you choose to socialise and who your friends are.

Online dating opens up a whole new world of people you wouldn't normally consider to date. Not because they're not nice people, but because you wouldn't normally come into contact with them. For example, the dating apps that allow you to discover men who have 'crossed your path' based on the locations stored on your phone have (mis) matched me with an array of traffic wardens, Uber drivers and binmen. This is simply because I have been in London on the same street as them at the same time, not because we are in any way suited.

Many of my dating stories stem from two people liking each other's photos and maybe a bit of a profile blurb. You could argue that this is no different to spotting someone in a bar then chatting them up. But in my experience the act of swiping right has often resulted in unrequited love.

I'm a normal girl, who was born to parents who gave me the best possible start in life. Mine were humble beginnings in a semi-detached home in Cambridge, but my dad's job as a journalist took us all over the world. I had a happy childhood, fantastic schooling and have always known I am loved. My mum was that idyllic mummy who stayed at home with us when we were little, taught us to read, tie our shoelaces and how to behave nicely. She was always there to play with us, pick us up from school, help with our homework and cook us delicious meals. The older I get, the more I find a new respect for my mummy and everything she did for us. My parents later divorced but they have always put me and my brother and sister first and brought us all up to be happy, independent and successful members of society.

Having had such a lovely upbringing, I always just assumed life would pan out fairly similarly for me. Get married, buy a house, have kids etc. Don't get me wrong: I cherish everything I have got but I'm trying to be better at the one thing I'm useless at – relationships with men!

For *The Man Detox*, I aim to bare my soul and elaborate on the good, the bad and the ugly. In order to get my head straight, I am going to try a self-imposed dating detox, starting with a month date-free. I discussed the possibility of three months with some of my closest friends and it felt too daunting. I have never gone three months without sex!

I have also *never* stuck to any kind of self-imposed restrictions in my life. I have mainly failed at any kind of self-imposed diet or fitness restrictions and I have a fuller figure. For example, while everyone was trying 'Dry January' and 'Veganuary' I tried NObreadUARY, a self-imposed (made up by me) ban on bread in January. Until I had a head-on collision with a sourdough loaf after just four days. I'm not saying bread is bad for you, per se, but I can't possibly have bread without butter, which in my case, equates to lardy hips.

But despite my inability to stick to rules, for some reason NOmenBER – that is, no men in November (another one made up by me) – felt doable and necessary. For this detox I set out a few rules:

1. No dates
2. No sex
3. No speaking to men who might be potential dates or sex

Over the month (maybe longer), while embracing all of these rules, I'm going to unravel my relationship history on a journey of self-discovery. I want to find out whether stopping dating altogether, while I reflect on my dating misdemeanours, as well as the loves of my life, will identify the reason for arriving at my single dead-end. I honestly feel exasperated by it all.

I have plenty of friends in the same boat. But I also have many friends who are 'living the dream'. Why have I not managed to achieve the doting husband, two kids, cottage in the Cotswolds, Land Rover Discovery and horses? OK, skip the horses... but where *is* he? I just want what so many 'successful' women in their late thirties seem to have achieved.

I'm hoping that by peeling back the layers of my dating back-catalogue, I can work out where/if I've been going wrong with the men I've met in my life. Has Mr Right already passed through, but slipped through the net? Have I been way too accommodating with the men I have dated who were never right for me in the first place? Have I been trying to find love through sex? Am I just not suited to modern dating in the digital world?

This is certainly not a dating tips book! By asking myself these questions while digesting my own dating stories, I'm hoping I can better understand me, myself and men. I don't think my dating stories are any worse, more extreme or funnier than anyone else's, but I am willing to lay myself bare and analyse them for the purposes of this experiment. I'm hoping that ultimately I can come up with a formula for moving forward. I'm not professing I will create a radical theory for a detox plan for others to follow, but I'm hoping I can make myself feel more empowered and may inadvertently help other people out of their dating cul-de-sac along the way.

As a bit of fun, but also by means of detoxing, I am going to include a song at the end of each chapter. Thanks to my parents' passion for music, particularly my mum, so many songs are particularly synonymous with certain people in my life for good and bad reasons. Working in radio for my whole career, I have had music pumping through my veins for most of my working day. We all have a soundtrack to our lives and music can immediately transport you back to a person, place, feeling, time in your life. Sometimes even the first few notes of a song can evoke these feelings. Which is why at the end of each chapter you will see a song for that person/time in my life.

Right, take a deep breath, get your tissues ready for laughter *and* sadness, and don't judge me... Get on board – it's time to start the Man Detox.

Chapter 2

Ignition

1 November

I came up with the idea for NOmenBER while I was chatting with two of my closest friends over coffee. I realised I had reached the end of my tether with dating. I was fresh from another 'funny', yet soul-destroying encounter with a man I had completely misjudged. You could say he was the straw that broke the camel's back. This toxic incident may have been a result of my willingness to see the best in everyone, my desperation to meet someone, or pure and simple naivety.

It was the previous month, not long after my thirty-ninth birthday and I was looking on the location-focused dating app Happn. I matched with a guy called Ronald, who described himself as a 'bodybuilding lawyer'. His photos lived up to the description. A good-looking black guy, with massive biceps, bursting out of his white-collar 'lawyer' outfit. We exchanged a few messages and discovered that we lived nowhere near each other. The only reason we 'happened' to match was because his train passed by my sister's house while I was visiting her. You could say it was fate, but it was also a bit creepy to think I was 'connecting' with someone simply on the basis he was whizzing past 'available' me. A bit like a satellite navigation system for singletons, haphazardly matching people on the basis that they are vaguely in same vicinity and are both looking for dates. What has the world come to?!

The name Ronald caused much hilarity among my friends and I got a barrage of texts asking 'When are you meeting Ronald McDonald? Hope he's not too much of a clown.' Ha-ha. Over the few perfunctory messages we exchanged he seemed nice enough, so I agreed to meet him for a drink in a pub halfway between us, as he lived a good hour from me. It was a freezing cold night, so I texted Ronald and offered to pick him up from the train station, as it was a ten-minute walk to the pub. I drove to the station in anticipation, but although he 'read' my WhatsApp message (I could see the two blue ticks) he didn't reply. I just thought I'd better stick to the plan of meeting him in the pub. Instead of doing that whole thing of sitting in the pub on my own waiting for him (and looking obviously as if I was on a first date), I waited in the car and phoned my mum.

I spoke, with deep sighs, about meeting yet another date, who I knew very little about, in the hope that he might be a potential perfect match. She gave me the usual pep talk about being careful, as I was meeting (yet another) complete stranger, off a dating app. My mum isn't averse to apps, and has been on a dating website herself, but she's always protective of me. 'You might be nearly forty, but you're still my baby.' As usual, I assured her I would text her when I got home.

While I was chatting to my mum, there was a group of guys who kept popping outside the pub to smoke. I didn't take too much notice, but they kept checking me out, making me feel quite silly about sitting in my car, which was getting more steamed up by the second on a freezing cold night. Eventually, a smart-looking black guy, who looked very like Ronald, turned up and walked into the pub. I walked in (heart pounding) and tentatively approached, crossing my fingers it was definitely him. He was much shorter than I imagined, but his muscles bulged just as much as his photos promised. We sat down and chatted very easily about ourselves, life and the universe.

He was a very interesting guy and we discovered that we both had siblings who worked as actors in the USA. He came from St Vincent and the Grenadines and regularly went back to see family. This made my ears prick up, that there might be a chance we could go and live in the Caribbean together one day (jumping the gun in my head as usual). But while we chatted very easily and laughed about the bizarre way we'd matched on Happn, there wasn't really any spark. I really wanted there to be something as he was a lovely guy and so smiley and friendly. But you can't force chemistry and we had about as much spark as two flames in the rain.

I was enjoying myself enough to repay him with a drink and he said he was happy with an orange juice. As I was standing at the bar, a very dapper looking chap in a suit and waistcoat started staring. I could see from the corner of my eye he was looking at me, but carried on with my order at the bar. He interrupted and said, 'Can I buy this drink for you?' I politely declined and turned away.

He struck up conversation again, 'Can I just say, you are a very beautiful woman. Please let me buy you a drink. Are you single?'

I whispered back, 'I'm actually on a date and these drinks are for him and me.'

He introduced himself, 'I'm Jay. What's your name? Go on, please let me buy these drinks for you.' I relented and said how weird it was that he was buying a drink for me and my date. He said, 'I saw you sat in your car earlier.'

I put two and two together and realised he was with the group of smokers who'd been staring at me in my in my car. I hadn't noticed him, but I was surprised I hadn't clocked him, as he was a good-looking guy. Turkish-looking with dark eyes and olive skinned and a thick Essex accent. He asked me, 'What's a good-lookin' girl like you doing on a date wiv 'im?' I got a bit defensive of Ronald and said that he was a nice guy, but it was only our first date. Jay said, 'Can I please take you out? I'm not a player. I don't do dating apps, I could take you on a much better date than 'ere. Go on, let me have your number, then if it doesn't work out, then let me take you out.' I reluctantly gave him my number, which he dialled straight away so I could save his number. He was beyond cocky and an absolute chancer with a glint in his eye. But I'll be honest: I was very flattered to be chatted up at the bar. It felt old-fashioned! No swiping left or right, just good old-school man-spots-woman-he-fancies-and-chats-to-her.

Ignition

I scuttled back to my actual date with Ronald and was relieved he had clearly been on his phone the whole time and was blissfully unaware of the whole conversation I had just had at the bar. We continued our evening and I dropped him back at the train station at the end of the night. There was a slightly awkward kiss. I had failed to notice he had incredibly dry lips and it was like kissing a tortoise's bottom. He said to me, 'The first date kiss is always so awkward.'

I just thought to myself, Yes, it can be, but you just made it even more awkward by saying that. He got out of my car and I *knew* that was probably the last time I'd ever see him or hear from him.

As I was driving home, I could hear my WhatsApp tinging away. I discovered a series of illiterate messages from an unknown number. It was Jay. I had effectively been on a date and got two-for-one. Talk about buses! He just reiterated everything he had said in the pub. 'All right SeXy its Jay your so sexy did i say that... so when i am taking U ouut?'

I thought to myself, he's either drunk or thick, as I messaged back: 'Nice to meet you, even though it was in slightly odd circumstances. Maybe we can chat on the phone first?'

'Yeh gonna phone ya.'

Meantime, despite our 'awkward' kiss, I didn't hear a peep from Ronald. I thought that was quite rude, as we'd had a nice evening. It wasn't my fault he needed some lip salve. But then I had a sinking feeling that maybe he *had* seen me talking to Jay at the bar after all. I guess I'll never know and, if I'm honest with myself, even if he'd had the softest lips imaginable, I still wouldn't have truly fancied him, I just fancied a life in the Caribbean.

The next day, Jay phoned me, as promised. I like it when a man actually picks up the phone and makes an effort to speak to you. So often these days, guys just reply on messages. But when your written English isn't great, chatting over the phone is a whole lot easier. He was *very* Essex and he made me feel very posh. But my family are from Essex, so I'm used to the accent. On the phone he was charming, wanting to stress he was old-fashioned when it came to dating and knew how to treat a lady. He told me he had been a semi-pro boxer and was very into his training, but had got out of shape a bit in recent times.

When I asked about his current profession, he said he was a 'classic car dealer' and ran his own workshop 'doing up nice little motors'. It wasn't something I was particularly interested in or knew anything about but I asked him all about it and let him chat away to me about his various 'little beauties' he'd bought, upgraded and sold on for a profit. After a few nights of him calling me, he said he'd be in my area to 'pick up some retro wheels', and asked if I wanted to meet. Seeing as Essex is at least an hour's drive away, it made sense to take advantage of an opportunity to meet in person although it was quick. But in my experience, it's never a good idea to have endless chats over the phone or over texts with a man: it's better to just meet and see if there is definitely some chemistry.

We arranged to meet in a nice little country pub about ten minutes from my house. What I had not realised in our first, five-minute chance encounter, was that this Essex charmer not only had more nervous energy than

Tigger from *Winnie the Pooh* but also absolutely no filter. He came bounding towards me as I sat on a sofa in a quiet corner of the pub opposite an elderly couple. He shouted, 'All wight, gorgeous, what ya drinkin'?' He lunged at me and manhandled me, with a firm hug and slobbery kiss on the cheek.

Inside the first ten minutes he told me, 'I well fancy ya, I knew I would, but you could do with losing a few pounds and should get down the gym, but I still fancy ya.'

In my head I was thinking, Whaat?! So I said, 'That is pretty rude. Shall I just leave right now?' He insisted it was just 'banter' and I 'shouldn't get sensitive'.

Inside I was thinking, *Ouch*. I was no different to the girl he met at the bar the week before. Maybe I had been wearing a more flattering outfit? Maybe he just saw me in a good light as I was buoyant from my nice date with Ronald? He went on, 'You just just need a bit of help with getting down the gym. I'll sort you out, we'll get you a training programme sorted.' It was like I was one of his classic cars: 'Yeah, I'll sort you out... couple of previous owners... check under the bonnet... pump up the tyres... lick of paint... you'll be good as new.'

He described the way he 'helped mates out' with deals. I didn't pry too much into what these deals were, but they seemed to be more than just car-related. He talked about getting 'high' a lot and couldn't believe it when I told him I was not interested in 'doing gear'. I grew up with the shock of Leah Betts, the girl who died after taking ecstasy, hitting the headlines, which was enough to put me off ever touching drugs. There was also a lot of chat about his mates 'doing time', like it was a rite of passage.

He basically lived a life of ducking and diving to make a living. He talked about wanting to settle down and start a family.

I was thinking, Not with me, mate! He asked me very little about me, as he was too busy talking (boasting) about himself. The number of boxing titles he had won, how he had made 'big' money but lost it all. He kept saying, 'You ain't ever gonna meet no one like me,' and I definitely believed that, but for all the wrong reasons. I couldn't quite believe that he was the same chap who I'd been speaking to over the phone for the past week. A seemingly cheeky guy, with a big personality and lots of love to give, turned out to be uncouth, rude and shady. We had gone from having an original spark at the bar the week before, to discovering we had absolutely nothing in common.

I felt embarrassed to tell him I had spent four years at university and had gone on to have a successful career as a broadcast journalist, having travelled the world and conducted high-profile interviews and broken important news stories. These facts about myself seemed boastful and irrelevant when all he wanted to talk about was the latest 'retro' car he had just bought. Which incidentally looked like a complete banger to me, ready to be scrapped, not 'done up'.

And yet I didn't get up and leave. In fact, I just nervously laughed it off. Why? Why didn't I stand up for myself when he told me to 'Lose a few pounds'? Why didn't I tell him to 'Fuck off' and walk out? Instead, I stayed for the rest of the date. I ate dinner with him, I heard his inane stories and watched his lack of decorum (he used the word 'cunt' like it was going out of fashion and ate with his mouth open, spraying his meal all over me – yuck).

I had worked out this date/potential relationship was not going anywhere. He asked me to 'keep an eye' on his wheels while he 'took a piss' and I told him there was absolutely no way I was going to stand anywhere near this untaxed heap of shite which he had revved up with thick black smoke coming out of the exhaust. I had thought he was a rough diamond but when he grabbed hold of me in the middle of the street, shoved his tongue down my throat and whacked me on the bum, I realised he was just rough. I made my excuses about needing to get home and as I walked off I said, 'You are never going to meet anyone like me.'

Needless to say, forty-one-year-old Jay, the 'Essex charmer', formed a big part of my decision to do this man detox. I really don't need wounding comments and behaviour like that in my life. I'm not trying to demonise Jay, but I do admit that I had accepted new lows by staying on the date despite his comments. It's not like he hit me, it's not like he stole from me, but he shattered my self-esteem. It was only in the days following that I realised this.

Maybe this was even one of my reasons for crying today, like my tears were purging his poisonous comments. I think crying will form a big part of this journey. But I can already feel the relief from writing down this story about Jay, as I can now laugh at it. I also feel like I have him to thank in some respects, as he was the 'ignition' (excuse the car pun) I needed to force me into the man detox. Also, I can't help but wonder if I should have sent Ronald a message instead of Jay. Did I look a gift horse in the (dry) mouth and go for the flattering naughty boy at the bar too easily? I think I have always gone for naughty boys too easily, which is maybe why I am single.

ARTIST: MC Hammer
TITLE: 'You Can't Touch This'
REASON: Self-explanatory! Jay can't touch this!

Chapter 3

No need to Block You

In the first few days of the man detox, like anyone trying to 'give up' something, I can barely think about anything else.

I mull over why it hasn't worked out with certain men and also feel uneasy about the fact I am stopping myself from having any contact or intimacy with men. I have been to the cinema to keep myself busy (saw *First Man* – good, but nothing particularly romantic). However, tiny little challenges crop up in day-to-day life. I had to ask my sister to turn off Jorja Smith, as her songs remind me too much of my recent love, Ben. Funny what emotions music can evoke, but then again, it was only ten days ago I told him I couldn't see him any more.

I was introduced to Ben by a friend. It was the previous New Year's Eve and I was meeting Lucy's new man, Adam, for the first time. We were celebrating the start of the new year at a country house, full of pompous, smug married couples and it was one of those occasions where I felt the 'nakedness' of being single. In my normal life, I don't think about it that much but when you have to hold your own at an event full of couples holding hands, dancing face-to-face, legs entwined and smooching as the clock strikes midnight, the stark reality that you are entering yet another year on your own makes you feel completely alone and deafened by other people's happiness.

Adam was adorable with all of us, bearing in mind he was entering a group of women who on the face of it were like *The Witches of Eastwick*. Highly successful businesswomen who have all been single for a while and were fairly sceptical about whether this new man was good enough for their Lucy. She can be a bit of an ice queen, but even though their relationship was only a few months old we could see Adam had melted her. Adam was a therapist and had a very spiritual side, which I could tune into. People always say I have an 'aura', which basically means I'm warm and transparent, and I am always drawn to spiritual people. Within hours of meeting, Adam had sussed me out, heard me moan about *still* being single at the age of thirty-eight and volunteered the information, 'You would love my mate Ben.' I blushed at the thought of being introduced to his best mate, but he phoned him immediately and gave the handset to me. 'Verity, Ben wants to talk to you'. We chatted away about nothing for a few minutes, with him laughing at everything I said about how it was so embarrassing that Adam was trying to set us up. Ben had a lovely soft voice, was so easy to talk to and sounded utterly charming. So that was New Year's Eve, but we didn't actually speak again or meet until the end of April.

No Need to Block You

It was 28 April, Saturday night and a few of us planned to go out in central London. We started off at Lucy's house with some cocktails and I got to meet Ben for the first time. He was exactly as Adam had described: 'in great shape', with huge muscles from working hard at the gym, around five feet nine inches, with a kind, smiley face. I immediately fancied him and had butterflies. We had an instant connection, knocking back the prosecco while I held court with our group, telling them about my week of the usual disastrous dating stories.

I was fresh from having had a Bumble app date, after which I had received a message on Twitter from someone who turned out to be my date's girlfriend, telling me she suspected he was two-timing her. (That's a whole other story for later in the book.) As I was telling this story, I was mindful of the fact I was essentially being set up with Ben for the first time and didn't want him to think I was some kind of dating hussy! I could tell he fancied me, even though he was not overtly flirty at first. He had 'that look' in his eyes that told me he liked me. I could feel him looking at me when I was gesticulating.

What is 'that look'?! It gets your heart sizzling, makes you blush and gets the blood pumping around your body, sometimes leaving you with slightly wet knickers. I suppose, if I could identify what that look was and could bottle it, I would be a millionaire. Ben definitely had a glint in his eye and a gaze that got me super-excited and gave me a green light to flirt.

The problem was, I didn't really know if Ben was definitely single. I knew from Adam that he had a long-term girlfriend, but it was 'complicated'. He also had a teenage daughter and immediately showed me photos of her. She was clearly his pride and joy and he totally adored her. I was aware that I needed him to take the lead with the flirting – at the grand old age of thirty-eight, you've learned that if a guy likes you, he will let you know. We left Lucy's house around 10 p.m. and we were all pretty merry.

In the back of a black cab, Ben made a point of sitting next to me. By the time we finished our fifteen-minute journey to Soho, he had been touching my leg and was holding my hand. Very subtly at first, but then when we got out of the cab he continued to hold my hand down the street and into the bar. He made me feel so feminine with his big, strong hands, gently touching the small of my back as we entered the bar. He knew the owner and we were immediately welcomed with free drinks and a VIP area and allocated a bucket-full of bottles of vodka, gin, whisky, wine, prosecco and mixers. A lethal concoction, when we had already had so much to drink at Lucy's. But we had a blast!

We drank and danced the night away, while I chatted nose-to-nose with Ben and eventually started snogging him at the bar, hiding from the rest of the group like naughty schoolkids. He was so sensual and had the most amazing lips I had ever kissed, soft and plump. Not too much forceful tongue, but enough to let me know he was interested. He had such a commanding touch, gently holding my waist, neck, back of my head and hair as he kissed me, making me go back for more and more. I could feel his hard cock pressing up against my inner thigh. We kissed passionately and the deafening music and bustle of the bar was almost muted/put on pause while we held each other.

No Need to Block You

By the end of the night, we were hammered and it was all a bit of a blur. I remember getting back to Lucy's and being in the hallway outside of her apartment, lying on the floor (!) with Ben, more enveloped in each other's bodies. We kept our clothes on but we must have looked like two rampant dogs, intertwined on the floor, but aged thirty-eight and forty-five. Not clever. So when Adam found us and barked at Ben to go home, I felt like a naughty teenager who had broken her curfew. But Adam was right: Ben needed to go home and I needed to go to bed. Especially as I still didn't know the status of his relationship.

I woke up the next day with one of *the* worst hangovers I have ever had. One of those that makes you promise you'll never drink again, while frequenting the bathroom all day and craving salty snacks around 4 p.m. when your body is empty and in need of carbs to restore some normality. I also had the regret about what I had done the night before with Ben. His touch was like no other. But he still shared a home with the ex-girlfriend he'd been with for twenty-five years and had a thirteen-year-old daughter. Despite his hinting he would be leaving the family home soon, I had been playing tonsil-hockey with a man who was not entirely available. In our drunkenness we had failed to exchange numbers and although Adam had introduced us, there was no way I was going to be the one to ask for Ben's number. I just put it all down to a bit of fun.

The problem with that conclusion was our respective best friends, Adam and Lucy, were a couple. It was only a matter of time before Ben and I were at the same event again. A few weeks after that fateful night it was Lucy's birthday and she planned a fabulous BBQ in the garden of her sister Bonnie's house in Maida Vale, London. It was a gorgeous summer's evening and ten of us sipped champagne and cocktails and ate delicious food. As I was busy nattering to the girls, Ben walked in and my heart skipped a beat. I knew there was a chance he would be coming to the party, but it wasn't a guarantee. He was looking as handsome as ever. Wearing a tight white T-shirt and jeans, he again gave me 'that look' and made me all of a flutter. Although Adam had introduced us, he was ribbing us the whole evening that we needed to be 'kept apart' after last time. He kept saying, 'You two can't be trusted.' It was funny but also hurtful, as Adam was making me feel like I had thrown myself at Ben and in my mind it takes two to tango.

I had occasional conversations with Ben, but it wasn't until the end of the night that we spoke properly. In fact, we had never really spoken properly, because the last time we had been insanely drunk! We discovered we have a really similar taste in music, mainly soul and R&B. Throughout the evening I was playing some of our favourite old-skool tunes from the '90s like Brownstone, Donell Jones and Aaliyah, with me shouting, 'Do you remember this one?' across the room while Ben pointed his finger in the air and shouted 'Tuuune!' I am incredibly passionate about music, and when I meet someone who has the same interest and the same taste, it's another connection. (But it also makes it incredibly hard to listen to that music if you split up with that person further down the line.)

At the end of the night, we were the last men standing – well, sitting, to be precise – while laughing and drinking copious amounts of rosé. This was easy, this was just two people getting on brilliantly, but then we started kissing. It was like landing back on a bed of pillows – the softest, warmest landing I could wish for. This was his lips gently pressing up against mine for the first time since the end of April. I had forgotten what an amazing kisser he was. So passionate and genuine.

I had arranged to stay at Bonnie's house and I suggested that we took our wine to the basement bedroom where I was staying, so we didn't disturb anyone else sleeping. Bonnie's house was unbelievably beautiful and the bedroom was like a five-star hotel. I dimmed the lights and put the music back on (low) and we carried on kissing on the bed. We carried on drinking and it was so nice to be with Ben while we were both *compos mentis*.

He was incredibly gentle but had a firm grip at the same time, as his hands explored my body and started to take my clothes off. We were soon both in our underwear, with me soaking wet and him rock hard. But there was still an element of 'Should we or shouldn't we?' Why had Adam been so adamant that we stay away from each other? Was Ben holding back from getting out his hard cock because he knew he shouldn't be doing anything with me if he was still in a relationship? We ended up having no-sex sex, where we satisfied each other but without intercourse.

By the beginning of August we had started meeting up regularly; having coffees and getting to know each other better. The sex was amazing from the word go – after having been with so many fuckers, although it sounds cheesy, it was refreshing that he wanted to make love to me. It wasn't the first time that I'd found a man who had been in a long-term relationship tended to be much better at making love as opposed to just fucking. He took his time, caressing every inch of me and making sure I was satisfied before he was. The problem was, it was making me fall for him. With both a sexual connection and a friendship bond, feelings start to run deep.

I quizzed him on whether he would be leaving the marital home anytime soon so we could be in a proper relationship, but he just brushed it off every time by saying, 'The ex and I live independent, separate lives under the same roof, but it's complicated.' I understood. He had his daughter to think about, but she will understand one day that mummies and daddies can fall out of love. I also understood that it was possible for a mummy and a daddy to remain friends. After twenty-five years together that connection is solid. I also felt a degree of sisterhood – I didn't want to be 'stealing' another woman's man if he wasn't definitely available.

I adored Ben and I wished I could be with him, but after six months of toing and froing he had still not proved to me that he wanted to be with me enough to make the leap and leave her for me. After six months of us sneaking around (so he didn't upset his daughter) I felt like his dirty little secret. Ben and I still had an amazing connection, which we both recognised, especially in the bedroom. But I have had Lucy and Adam and all of our mutual friends quizzing us repeatedly, 'What's going on with you two?'

After many tears, I spoke to him ten days ago and I told him I couldn't carry on like this. I told him I deserved better than to be someone's bit on the side. He agreed, but he still didn't say he was going to change anything. That was his chance! That was his chance to say, 'Verity, I want to be with you, I will do what it takes to make that happen.' I was crying my eyes out while I was on the phone to him, which I was cross about, but I couldn't help it. I told him I was sad that we couldn't continue seeing each other, but we left things on very amicable terms.

We have exchanged a few messages since, but this story forms one of many reasons why I came to the decision that I needed to do the man detox. My sister suggested I just block Ben on my phone. That way, if he messaged me I wouldn't even know about it. What I don't know won't hurt me, and all that. But for now, this quote summed up how I feel: 'No need to block you, I want you to see what you lose.'

ARTIST: Jorja Smith
TITLE: 'Tomorrow'
REASON: This song and the album are synonymous with my relationship with Ben, as we listened to it together.

Chapter 4

Going for the Loaf

Today I had a great day at work. These occasions need to be celebrated, as they don't happen every day. I was nominated for an award recognising my achievements in radio and this has reminded me why I need to not only strive for excellence in my work but also in my relationships.

For the past seven years (actually, nearly eight) I have had a fuck buddy (FB). I met him at a friend's party in February 2011. It was a ski party, so everyone was dressed up in skiwear, apart from me, as I have never been skiing and don't have any ski-wear. Plus, I felt insecure enough about looking fat, without adding extra padding in the form of puffy jackets and Salopettes!

The party was held by a girl I had met through work; I didn't know many people there, although we did have a few mutual friends. We were in a moodily lit pub with lots of people darting out to smoke on a freezing

February night. I had taken a friend who didn't know anyone and when she showed signs of wanting to leave we ordered a cab.

While we were waiting near the door, I bumped into a gorgeous, strapping black guy who I almost chest-bumped coming in. I was a bit taken aback, but he was absolutely gorgeous and I'll never forget my cheesy but inadvertently successful chat-up line – 'Where have you been all night?' I meant it! He was so handsome and I hadn't seen him until the last minute. We chatted briefly and he asked for my number.

Little did I know that chance meeting would develop into my longest (non) relationship. He was James from east London and I'd barely got back home before he texted and told me he wanted to come over right away. Despite the briefness of our first encounter, I knew I wanted to see him again, but by then I was in my pyjamas without any makeup: there was no way he was coming then. Plus, I wanted to go on a date with him! You know, lunch, a drink, the cinema – a normal, nice date. I told him I was free the next day and we agreed to do Sunday lunch. Fabulous! All I've ever wanted is a handsome man to walk down Clapham High Street with, arm in arm, heading for a cosy Sunday roast. I've watched enough other smug couples do that over the years!

I remember the following day I waited on the sofa at 2 p.m. However, 2 p.m. came and went. I was still in my coat at 3 p.m. I was lying on the floor in despair between 4 p.m. and 5 p.m. By 6 p.m. I was in floods of tears, in the foetal position, on the floor, being comforted by my housemate. *This* should have been enough of a red flag. But instead, in usual Verity fashion, I gave him the benefit of the doubt when he eventually got in touch to say his grandma had been ill. The irony is that he has gone on to use the 'ill Grandma' excuse many times over the years – I think she's died about three times!

I eventually calmed down and, after he'd apologised profusely, we went on our first date, for lunch in my local pub. I remember him standing behind me at the bar, placing a firm grip over my arse-cheek, telling me, 'There's a lot of junk in that trunk and I like it.' It was so sexy to have his big hands on my body in such a public environment.

We went back to my house, but I said I wasn't going to sleep with him so early on after meeting him. He barked at me, 'Why did you invite me back here then, if you're not going to have sex?'

I responded, 'I'm not that kind of girl.'

Instead, we started kissing on my bed and he soon started pushing my head down towards his cock. This was one of my first encounters with a cock that was too big for my mouth. I remember my dentist telling me once that I had a small mouth and without realising what I was saying, retorted with, 'I've never had any complaints.' God knows what he thought!

I went to the pub with my girls a few days later and in true *Sex and the City*-style girls chat, I told them about James. 'Oh my God, you'll never guess what. I met this guy at a party this other week, and he came back to my place this week, and he had *the* biggest cock I have ever seen...' Straight away, they wanted to know how big he was, so I reached for the nearest demonstrative implement I could find and it happened to be a giant candle sat in the pub table. I described to great hilarity how I could barely fit this man's huge, girthy cock in my mouth. I had also never really experienced sucking a man who was almost flaccid and feeling him get more and more erect while he was inside my mouth, but that's what he wanted and it made it easier to fit him in, initially. The girls rolled about with laughter as we christened him Mr Candle Cock. They also wanted to know whether I would see him again and whether it was the start of a beautiful thing.

I think at first I tried to kid myself that it might be. There's a reason I make the comparison with *Sex and the City*, as it was a major part of my age group's sexual conditioning. It completely normalised my behaviour and that of my friends when it came to sex. In my group I have always been the more of the outrageous sex-fiend Samantha. So it came as no surprise to them I had snared myself a gorgeous black model and personal trainer with a giant cock.

I fancied the pants off him, but I didn't really like him as a person, which I was never going to admit to the girls. He hadn't been that nice to me: not showing up for our first date, forcing my head down on his cock, and getting cross with me because I wouldn't sleep with him on our first date. However, I liked having him in my bed, as he looked good. Terrible! My expertise in the blow-job department soon developed into sex. The good thing was, he wasn't very good at lasting very long. It was selfish of him, but I could forgive him as I couldn't physically handle him inside me for that long.

It soon became clear that James was not the relationship type. He had *never* been in a fully committed relationship and, to this day, I don't think he knows how. He had two young daughters, who were months apart from different mothers. Fortunately, he had decided early on that he wanted to be a good dad and be there for them. This did, however, set the scene for what I was getting into: a man who did not commit to anyone or anything. Pretty early on, I took it for what it was. Sex with a very hot man with a six-pack, a massive cock and no strings attached. However, this casual sex has gone on and on and on and on and on, and in the blink of an eye, eight years have gone past. I have made it way too comfortable for him. He would come over in the afternoon, have some food, have sex, have a sleep and watch TV. It was indulgent for both of us and we both got something out of it sexually. Initially I fell for him, as I thought he was playing hard to get, but actually he was just being James.

I have no idea what he gets up to from one week to the next. He is a self-confessed womaniser. But every time we meet, on average once a month, he has given me a reason to get waxed, shave my legs, wash my sheets and make myself feel nice to get ready for a man in my bed. Pathetic really, but I have spoken to other people about the perks of having a 'friend with benefits' and as long as you have the ability accept it for what it is and compartmentalise feelings for them, it's mutually agreeable. I also got a lot out of him sexually. It's not just men who enjoy casual sex.

I have often wondered whether living with my gay housemate Steven also normalised the arrangement. Steven had many partners while we lived together and we always joked that we had a revolving front door, like you see in a grand hotel, with such a large number of men coming and going through it. And Steven would ask, 'Is today a James day?' when he saw me suddenly cleaning and tidying the flat.

It wasn't all about the sex either. Sometimes James would just kiss me from head to toe. Who doesn't love that on a rainy Tuesday afternoon? He loved to tell me what was going on in his world, offload what was stressing him out about work and his girls. Over the years we have been there through the highs and lows of each other's careers and lives. I have had relationships in that time, but ultimately I've always known James was there, if I let him come round.

He's also never stopped me meeting other men, as there have been times when I've had to tell him I'm 'not available right now' and he would get it. But you could also say he has used me, as there have been times when we've arranged to see one another and he has just not turned up for hours, if at all. It's as if he likes to check he's still got me where he wants me. This is a complete disrespect of my time and I should have been mad at him, but for some reason I have always forgiven him and just made the most of seeing him, whenever.

This is what a friend of mine calls 'taking the crumbs' when I should be 'going for the loaf'. This is particularly true as James has effectively been breadcrumbing me for nearly *eight years* – otherwise known as stringing me along. I am going to keep typing 'eight years', so that I come to terms with that fact during this man detox. My time with James was never going to be anything more than sex, so why did I accept it? I can tell you. He is gorgeous. I fancied the pants off him. We got on well. And it was easy.

Going for the Loaf

Some may argue there is not a problem with casual sex. But I honestly don't think it has helped with my quest for a happy, life-long relationship and hopefully kids someday.

James has been my dirty (big) secret for too long and too much of a gap-filler. Whenever I've been in bars, at parties or sports clubs or on an online date – i.e. somewhere there may have been the potential to meet someone decent – I haven't always tried, as I've known James would always be there to fall back on. James doesn't know that I'm doing this man detox, so for him it's a bit confusing that I'm suddenly not replying to his messages about 'catching up'. I'll work out a way of telling him why we can't see each other for sex any more, but I know he's not going to like it.

We have had our frivolous, eight-year chapter and I don't want to go back to that. Today, I have been reminded that I am good at my job, by being nominated for excelling in my field. This is because, when it comes to my job, I always strive for the best, aim for the stars and go for gold. Which has reminded me, I need to do the same in my relationships too.

ARTIST: Chris Brown
TITLE: 'Fine China'
REASON: James once picked me and swung me around while dancing to this song.

Chapter 5

Daddy's Girl

I believe positivity is a mindset and that you can train yourself to be positive. For some reason, I am pretty much always positive, a glass-half-full kind of girl and I think this is hereditary. Today I went for a walk with friends in Richmond Park in London and when we arrived it was pouring, but I was absolutely adamant the rain would clear and the sun would come out in time for our walk... and it did!

I've realised I need to apply my positivity to every area of my life. I feel very blessed in many ways, but I think I may have soaked up a bit of my mum's less-than-sunny disposition when it comes to men. And I can't help but feel she kind of enjoys seeing me do this man detox, as she says of men, 'They're all a waste of space.' My dad has a lot to do with why I am the way I am too. I had a lot of rejection from him and as I try to reassess who I am and where I'm at with my relationship history, I can't ignore how much my dad has shaped my view of men.

From the word go, I was a daddy's girl. I would follow him around the house as a toddler, go to cricket and football matches with him from the age of three. He would strap me to the back of his bike, on a precarious makeshift saddle, with a lack of awareness of health and safety only acceptable in the '80s. I remember always wanting to please him, wanting him to be proud of me. Writing him stories, painting him pictures. If I was ever naughty, I would always write him a grovelling sorry letter or love letter:

Dear Daddy, I am sooo sorry for being rude, please forgive me, I won't do it again. I will tidy my room, wash the dishes and clean out Hoppy [my rabbit]. I am so sorry again, love you,

Vxoxoxoxoxoxxoxox

I can even remember the red-and-black, heart-shaped notepaper I used. Looking back, both my mum and dad were very young when they were firefighting with parenting, and my dad will admit that he probably did get a bit too cross with me and my brother at times. But my parents were almost kids themselves! They got married and had me by the time they were twenty-four, followed by my brother only eighteen months later.

This meant they were guessing when it came to discipline and some of their parenting was somewhat Victorian, harking back to the way they were brought up by my elderly grandparents. We weren't allowed to leave the dinner table until we finished our dinner. Smacking wasn't out of the question if we were really naughty, nor was getting grounded for answering back or being cheeky. All perfectly OK disciplinary action back then. Nowadays kids probably take out high court injunctions against parents for that kind of behaviour!

I remember being extremely proud of telling my friends at school that my dad was a newspaper editor. We lived all over the place as I was growing up, including Hong Kong, and I used to say I was half-Chinese as I thought I became half the nationality based on the fact I'd lived in Hong Kong! Funny how a child's mind works. I think my distinctly Caucasian, blonde hair, blue eyes and milk bottle-white skin were enough of a giveaway!

My dad's high-powered job meant that he wasn't always around, due to working nightshifts and long hours. Daddy was put on a pedestal as he wasn't around as much as Mummy, and I longed for his attention. He was very tactile, considering my granddad wasn't the cuddly type and like often breeds like. He was always ready to play dad-type boisterous games with me and my brother. He had high expectations we would be independent and confident individuals from the word go.

I remember when he took the stabilisers off my bike. Instead of steadily taking me out on just two wheels for the first time, he just took me to the top of a hill and pushed me, insistent I would be fine. I had two choices – fly down the hill and keep pedaling or fall off. This was fairly representative of his tough love at times. Always there to give me a push in the right direction, but not necessarily there to support me along the way. Get your feet off the ground and go and make something of yourself. So I did!

When it comes to genetics, I am fascinated with how

much of our personality is due to nurture and how much is down to nature. I am very close to my mum these days, but I am still very much like my dad in personality. I am creative, affectionate and have a vivacious personality. Slightly less attractive traits include being impatient, ridiculously clumsy and getting itchy feet very easily. I am a journalist like my dad, so my creativity and willingness to write and broadcast stories comes from him, although we have gone into very different fields in our shared profession.

I also have the Geere trait of being able to 'park' feelings and 'box off' those parts of my life I don't wish to dwell on. This doesn't mean I've swept those parts of me under the carpet, but that I've found a way of reconciling my feelings over something hurtful, like my parents' divorce. I was aged twelve when they split, my world fell apart and my family life changed beyond recognition. I was still playing with dolls and prams, making jam tarts and having vaguely adult thoughts about Laurence Oliver (always wanting to play kiss-chase with him more than anyone else). But essentially, I was an extremely naive twelve-year-old. My mum sat me down to tell me my dad had 'met another woman'. I remember I didn't understand what that meant at first. Why was it a big deal, that he had met another woman?

Then I started to understand why my mum was crying and screaming at my dad. To this day it remains one of the most traumatic periods of my life. My mum went mental – she was drinking and shouting. But it was soon apparent that my mum had not been entirely innocent herself and had also had affairs. But she maintained that she hadn't left my dad as a result of her misdemeanours. She drummed it home that my dad was incredibly selfish for running off with his 'bit of stuff'.

At first, the situation after they went their separate ways was novel. I had another place to go at weekends and see my dad. I asked him what 'the other woman' was like and he told me she had purple hair and ate chocolate for breakfast. Which I thought was really cool. Such a weird thing to be impressed by. I knew other kids at school whose parents were divorced, but I remember being *so* embarrassed mine had split up too. My perfect family had been split in two.

My dad moved to Canada and America in my teens, which I thought would be exciting for us, but it just meant I saw even less of him. He wasn't around to do all the hard parenting of the teenage years. He just flew us out to see him for the holidays and spoilt us. I had to re-connect with him each time and learn to cope with him devoting himself to my step-mum and not me. But in having to compete for his attention, I always felt rejected. It also meant that the daddy-daughter relationship transitioned into one in which we were more like friends. Which brings me to where I am today.

At the age of thirty-nine I can safely say that being mates works for us. He will never be there for me to spill my heart out about relationships. He used to call my long-term boyfriend David, 'ya friend David'. We can have hour-long chats and completely avoid the dreaded subject of 'love life'. He's good with professional advice, anything to do with home stuff and generally pushing me in the right direction if I need to make any decisions. Rather than seeing his absence as representing rejection and him being unsupportive (as with the day he took me on my bike to the top of the hill without my stabilisers), I just see him doing his best at being a dad, trying to give me the confidence to get on with it and make something of myself in many situations. He's now deaf, so we use Facetime rather than chat over the phone. It amazes me how he has coped with losing one of his senses almost overnight, and yet remains so positive about everything.

While I try to use this man detox to offload, digest and reassess where I am with men, I think it's fair to say I've often hankered after the love and affection I craved/missed from my dad. I've lapped up male attention in the most extraordinary situations and I've also pursued scenarios involving men in which I can avoid rejection by keeping the relationship casual. I've tried to settle for someone who's not right for me and also attempted to fit my round self into a square hole, just for the sake of a relationship. But now I'm older and wiser, I can see that my dad left my mum, not me. Also, now I've written about my dad, it's enabled me to recognise that it's thanks to him I can also grab hold of the positives in most situations and whiz down the steep hill of life, just 'getting on with it'.

ARTIST: Level 42
TITLE: 'Running in the Family'
REASON: Totally takes me back to listening to Level 42 in the back of the car with my mum and dad.

Chapter 6

Eww de Toilette

My aim in this man detox has not been to put myself off men altogether, but this weekend I have been away filming with two boys (one gay, one straight and attached) and they've done a pretty good job of reminding me how gross men are! They consistently sniggered about 'dropping the kids off' (going to the toilet), walked their filthy, muddy boots through the B&B (which I was left to vacuum) and were happy to leave their dirty pants strewn across the bedroom floor. This is standard male behaviour but unless you are in love with that man, it's just... eww.

One of the loves of my life in recent years was testament to the old saying, 'Love is blind' and, in his case, nose-blind too. I met Pete at work. When he first started working with me, I honestly remember seeing him walk through the door and being a bit scared of him. He wasn't famous, but he looked it. He had long, blond hair halfway down his back and a permanent scowl. He embraced a stereotypical

43

scruffy rocker look, with a leather jacket, black jeans, black rock-band T-shirts and heavy, buckled ankle boots.

One day, I got talking to him in the kitchen making coffee. From there we started emailing each other across the office. The emails were innocuous at first, until one day I could feel him upping the ante with his comments about my appearance and the clothes I was wearing. He was not a scary, moody-looking monster after all. Instead he was flirty and warm, and I started to see him more like a gorgeous Disney hero with flowing locks, like John Smith in *Pocahontas*.

It didn't take long to discover he was single. He had been married and had a young son, but after he had cheated on his wife they had started divorce proceedings. His affair had been short-lived and he told me it was his biggest regret, having ruined his marriage. He was no longer with the adulteress and had moved into the old bachelor pad he had bought before he got married. He commuted for four hours a day and stayed in a dingy hotel twice a week. The marriage split had left him financially screwed, with battered self-esteem, and in a very low place emotionally. He had become a bit of a loner, so when I popped up offering to make him drinks and get him a sandwich at lunchtime, I could tell he really appreciated someone being nice to him.

I offered to cook him dinner when he was staying in town and he jumped at the chance. I asked him what he liked to eat and without hesitation he suggested steak. I thought it was pretty cheeky, but I went ahead and bought a nice rump steak. He arrived at my house late in the afternoon and soon made himself comfortable on my sofa, stretching out his legs and suggesting I get him drinks and snacks. I would do this for any guest, but he was flirty and naughty with it. He stayed on the sofa bed that night and I remember spending the whole night wondering if I would get a knock at the door. Soon after this, he started to stay once a week.

After a few weeks of sofa-surfing, he cheekily lay on my bed 'for a rest'. He suggested that to help him relax, I might like to kiss the back of his neck. It was weird to move his long hair away from his neck and press my lips against his neck before kissing his actual lips, but I obliged. It was strangely sexy. I had always encouraged men to kiss me on the neck, so I understood why he liked it. He smelt very different to other men I had been with. It wasn't unpleasant, in fact it was strangely sexy and natural. It turned out that he was the closest I had ever got to a Neanderthal. He told me he didn't have a sense of smell and didn't believe in deodorant and liked to wash in water alone, showering without gel. He used shampoo for his hair infrequently and his body odour was 'all man'. In this day and age, it's unusual to meet people who aren't taking several bottles into the bath or shower and dousing themselves in perfumes, especially me. I love my smellies.

The neck-kissing soon turned into kissing everywhere and we discovered our chemistry transferred to the bedroom very easily. Apologies – potential nausea coming up... the thing was, his 'scent' was a lot to get used to. I remember going down on him for the first time and thinking, Oh lordy, just breathe in, it'll be fine. It was potent to say the least. He smelt very strongly of pheromones, a kind of gluey, creamy, cheesy scent. He didn't believe in any kind of manscaping. I like men to be manly, but there's nothing worse than getting forest-like, 'naturally' odoured, wiry pubes in your face, especially if they get stuck in your teeth. He had a great cock, girthy and long, but again it just didn't smell that fresh. But for some reason, I just accepted it as part of him, and weirdly, it was a real turn-on.

He soon started to stay two or three times a week. I gave him a key to my flat and without discussing it, we had sleepwalked into a full-blown, unofficial relationship, effectively living with each other half the week. I had booked to go away with my girlfriends that Easter and this was the first time I'd left him to his own devices in my flat. I remember lying by the pool in Portugal one day and receiving a Facebook message from him:

Hey. I know this will most likely annoy you and I'm already sorry. I wanted to write down some stuff for work so I just opened a drawer to see if there was a pad or something. I found a notebook. Perfect, there'd be some spare paper in there. I saw you had written some notes. Curiosity got the better of me. Stupidly in my low state of late, I thought it would be nice to see you say some nice things about me, if you said anything at all. Yes, I read the last passage. I'm sorry. You can hate me and if you want me to leave I will.

In truth I'm really upset. I feel pretty humiliated. I have told you everything. You have seen me at my worst and I've told you the truth. I've been so open with you. To know the things you have felt about me hurts, it really does and that's how I know I think a lot of you. The fact it does hurt.

I had no idea you thought I had hygiene issues. I feel so embarrassed. OK, I don't always wash my hair but I do try and keep myself clean ... everywhere. I'm sorry I don't meet your expectations and am not the person you hope for in life. I've been honest with you. You honestly could have done the same. I think the world of you. Your caring and kindness has been so nice and unexpected and I hope I can repay it someday. Right now I feel hurt and upset that you couldn't have told me about any issues or concerns you had about me.

Ironically, I have a piece of paper now, but have written nothing!

I'm sorry I read 'my' passage. My motivation wasn't distrust or even a blatant invasion of privacy. My battered confidence and self-esteem was looking for some niceness I hoped I might find.

I'm sorry again.

Love,

A humiliated and sad (again) Pete xx

To this day, this is one of the most excruciating messages I have *ever* received in my life. What he had found was something I had written in the early days of meeting him, when I was almost trying to put myself off him, as I knew he wasn't emotionally available.

I had listed 'The Bad Boys' with pros and cons attached to each name. In the notes attached to Pete, I had described in great detail what the downsides were to seeing him. Including: 'He smells like a farmyard animal and has the stinkiest cock I have ever sucked'. Total head-in-the-hands moment. Of course, I was angry he had abused my trust by reading my deepest, darkest secrets, especially as he would have needed to dig around deep in the drawers to find that particular notepad. More than anything, I was mortified he had read those comments as I never meant to hurt him. I never expected him to read it but, most of all, I didn't care enough about the odour to stop seeing him.

I apologised profusely for hurting his feelings and he said he was sorry for invading my privacy. We tried to put the whole saga behind us. But it had sowed a seed of doubt in his mind. He wasn't sure that I was serious about him and it became a classic case of him pulling away from me, which made me want him even more. The physical side effects of guilt combined with love were volcanic. It was one of the few times in my life when I could not physically stomach eating anything, as I felt such deep sorrow. I remember seeing him walk through the door at work and feeling so sick that I wanted to vomit my porridge back up immediately.

Also, him withdrawing from me had reminded me of what a life without him would be like. I became more and more addicted to him. Love is a drug after all. Every time my message notifications went ping it was like the sound bolted straight through me and I would physically shudder (pretty annoying when it was just Mum sending a message!).

He continued to stay at mine, letting himself in with his own key. But he could be quite moody at times and I never knew which Pete I was going to get. I usually stay in the same mood most of the time, apart from the odd teary 'time of the month'. They say women have menstruation moods, but I think men have monthly moods too sometimes!

Eww de Toilette

Soon after the diary incident, he came back to mine when I was in my room. I was lying on my bed reading and my heart was pounding so hard, it was like my heartbeat was pulsating through the mattress and my hands were trembling, as I anticipated him coming into see me. I was never not excited to see him. The build-up of seeing him at work, where he always ignored me like a complete stranger (so there was no suspicion about 'us'), left sexual tension between us. But on this occasion, I just heard the front door slam, followed by the lounge door shutting. Had he really just gone straight into the lounge without seeing me? Or was it someone breaking and entering my home?

Minutes passed and my heart was still going like the clappers, but I built up the courage to creep from my bedroom to the lounge of my maisonette. There he was, fast asleep across the length of my sofa, snoring his head off. I felt so violated that he'd had the audacity to come into my house with the key I had given him, but couldn't even be bothered to come and see me to say hello. He knew I was home! When I questioned him about it later, he claimed the sneaking into lounge was so that he didn't disturb me. He had been tired and just wanted to get his head down. When he explained it like that, it felt perfectly acceptable, but that occasion was a turning point as far as I was concerned.

Whenever he had come to my house up to that point, he would *always* come straight in to see me. The diary incident had decimated the respect between us. He had violated my trust by reading it, but he had also ruined his feelings for me and now he became a little dismissive. I desperately tried to cling on to what relationship we had by making him his favourite food all the time, even supplying him with his own treat box of his favourite chocolate bars, but the more I tried, the more I felt him pull away.

I even googled 'What do you do when a man pulls away?' but found little help available, just gossipy women's magazine articles suggesting, 'Keep yourself busy and be less available.' But I was fixated on Pete. I loved him so much I couldn't find any answers which helped my cause. I would lie in bed with him and he would just roll over instead of cuddling me. It's amazing how alone you can feel when you are sharing a bed with a man who doesn't want you. I would reach out and put my arm over him, but he would ignore me, pretending to be asleep. I would regularly cry myself to sleep next to him, snoring heavily, so desperate for him to love me. Instead I let him 'use' me whenever he needed to.

When we did have sex, it was mainly me sucking him off, getting on top and him loudly groaning his way to an orgasm, all in the space of fifteen minutes. It was almost perfunctory. It wasn't rape, as I consented every time, but I felt obligated to perform what he wanted in order to please him, all through my guilt. Looking back now, I realise that my willingness to open my legs and let him play with me when he wanted or fondle my boobs when he chose, was psychologically corrosive.

I also became obsessed with checking his social media activity. Who he interacted with, which posts he 'liked', 'shared' and 'retweeted'. It was like self-harming. For example, he was very active on Twitter and if I saw a scantily clad, tattooed girl tell him how gorgeous he was in reply to a Twitter post, I could feel a physical stabbing feeling in the heart EVERY TIME. It's making my heart pound now as I write about it.

This resulted in more self-harming in the form of getting together with another man. In May, the month after Pete read my diary, I got a message from an old fling called Greg. He was a struggling musician and would periodically pop up on my social media and 'like' my posts too. He had liked a photo on my Instagram and minutes later messaged to say how good I looked and asked what I was up to for the weekend. I told him I was going to a festival, which totally coincidentally he said he was going to be at too.

Greg and I ended up meeting at the gig and he came back to mine for a one-night stand. It was terrible sex, he was selfish and treated me like his 'warm hole' for the night, as he so lovingly described it. It was also terrible because I knew I was only doing it as revenge for the way Pete had been treating me. I suspected he was sleeping around behind my back due to his lack of interest in me and his heightened Twitter activity with a girl called 'Inky Lish' – the 'inky' referring to her tattoos. I wanted to play him at his own game. But I also felt tremendous guilt afterwards, as I didn't know for sure if he was definitely two-timing me. I had just decided that he was, judging by those clues.

Not long after, I remember sitting in the doctors, cursing Pete because I was suffering with cystitis. We had been having rigorous sex but because my head was distracted and the trust had gone, I hadn't been wet enough. If I am keen on someone and the chemistry is there, I never have a problem with being wet. Now the cystitis was killing me in weeing or even functioning normally. Even my legs ached and my head was all over the place.

Man Detox

I sat in the waiting room of the clinic, scouring Pete's Twitter, repeatedly stabbing myself in the heart seeing all the 'likes' from his gorgeous, adoring fans. Meantime, I beat myself up thinking, He has a key to my house, gets sex on a plate, gets his favourite food and treats me with contempt through the way he speaks to me. How did I get into such a toxic cycle of infatuation?

The Pete situation ran for eighteen months. I remember my nearest and dearest friends repeatedly saying, 'Are you *still* seeing that idiot?' but I was in love with him. I didn't care what anyone said. Eventually I happened to move away, which was an abrupt geographic and emotional separation.

When I think about his natural musk, his 'Eww de Toilette', I can, hand on heart, say I never worried about his scent and just accepted him as him. But I did go too far in accepting the way he treated me, on top of the fact he didn't smell fresh. I'm not going to actively seek out a man who doesn't shower, but it proves the point that if the chemistry is right, I will put up with men and their stinky ways. I loved him and love is blind and, on this occasion, like carbon monoxide – odourless and extremely toxic.

ARTIST: Eric Clapton
TITLE: 'Behind the Mask'
REASON: It always reminds me of Pete, as he played it to me.

Chapter 7

Fate, Full of Attraction

For me, one of the best things about my job as a journalist is the immediacy and quick turnover of the stories I cover, often on tight deadlines. It suits my short attention span.

I'm very embarrassed about this personality trait, but I was born with it and it makes many of my nearest and dearest think I'm not capable of sticking to my man detox. It's the same with everything in my life. I can never just watch TV: I always need to be doing something else at the same time, whether I'm cooking, cleaning, reading, typing or scanning socials. But I do also have the ability to think of something to say off the top of my head, which is effectively what co-presenting on the radio involves.

One day I answered a call in the newsroom from a panicked PR guy barking, 'You're booked in for a 10 a.m. ISDN.' He meant I was supposed to talk to someone down an ISDN line, a sophisticated sort of phone line, the quality of which makes it sound like you're in the same room when listeners hear the broadcast, although you and your subject can't even see each other. I didn't know anything about this interview. I looked at the clock and it was 10.10 a.m., so whoever was booked had already lost ten minutes of their slot.

I tried to calm him down. 'OK, well, I can do it. Who is it and what's the interview for?' I have had enough practice in my career to know my basic journalistic questions: 'Who?', 'What?', 'Where?', 'Why?', 'How?' and 'When?' will get me through subjects with anyone about anything.

The panicked voice started to ease. 'That's great, it's talking about his new movie, *Attack of the Wild Things*.' I was thinking, I have vaguely heard of him and this film, so I can do this no problem. 'Yep, that's fine, just let me have the ISDN and I'll dial you now.'

I ran into the studio, dialled the number, set the wave file to record, checked the levels and lifted the microphone:

ME: Hello, is that ... ?

JOSH: Yup. [sounding abrupt, as he had been waiting
        around for the interview]

ME: OK, great, thanks for your time today. Sorry
        about the delay, you're speaking to Verity Geere.

JOSH: Hi Verity Geere, great name. [sounding warmer]

ME: Thanks! So first of all, can you tell me a bit
        about yourself?

JOSH: Err... [guffawing] Well, if you *haven't* heard of
        me, I'm a comedian and I've just co-produced
        and starred in my first feature-length movie,
        Attack of the Wild Things.

Fate, Full of Attraction

ME: Great! Congratulations on your first movie. For anyone who hasn't seen the movie, can you give us a synopsis of what it's all about?

JOSH: Well, basically, it's about some birds who think they're human and start attacking London as they want to mark their territory, with comedic consequences.

ME: How is that funny?

JOSH: Have you seen the movie, Verity?

ME: Yeah, most of it. [I hadn't seen any]

JOSH: Well, maybe you missed the best bits, but it's fucking hilarious and you should go see it.

ME: Yes, I will. Can we leave out the swearing? As although this is pre-recorded interview, we can't risk having any swearing in the edit.

JOSH: Sure, sorry, miss. [sounding more cowardly]

ME: What were your favourite bits of the film?

JOSH: Oh God, err... so, there's this hilarious bit where the main bird, Manson, tries to gather up as many newspapers as possible and dive through a skyscraper with them in his beak.

ME: Well, in the current climate, how did you make sure this was tastefully done? [thinking on my feet, as it wasn't long after terrorist attacks in London and people were on high alert for anything crashing into skyscrapers. My question might make a good angle for news bulletins]

JOSH: Well, if you'd seen the flipping film, you would *know* that this was funny and not offensive in any way. [sounding more agitated]

55

ME: Well, I have seen most of it! [literally just realising I had actually seen the trailer] What was it like transforming yourselves into giant bird outfits every day?

JOSH: Really fucking hot. Oh, sorry, I forgot about the swearing thing. Yeah, hard going, spending three-to-four hours in costume and make-up ahead of each shoot.

ME: OK, what would you say to anyone thinking about seeing the film? [I was thinking, here's your last chance to really sell it, mate]

JOSH: If you fancy a laugh, seeing four idiots dressed up as giant birds try and take over the capital, then go see my new movie, *Attack of the Wild Things.*

ME: Brilliant, thanks for your time.

JOSH: Thanks Verity Geere ... Verity Geere ... I'm Verity Geere ...

I faded my microphone, but I could hear the cocky little twat repeating my name over and over again. I just chose to ignore it and put it down as a terrible interview not to be repeated. Admittedly, I should not have spoken to him without seeing the film, but he was such an arsehole. I came out of the studio, shell-shocked by what had happened and whispered in my colleague Anna's ear: 'I just did one of *the* worst interviews of my life.' I explained why.

'He was probably just in the middle of a junket day,' she said, meaning that he was likely going from one interview to the next for hours, with each media outlet asking the same questions, 'and totally sick of trying

flog his dead-horse film.' We laughed it off and forgot
about it.

Two days later, I went out in Peckham, to a dead-end pub
for a friend's birthday. For some reason the chosen drink
for us girls that night was Campari, which meant I was
very merry, very quickly. It was the summer and we were
all dressed in light dresses and strappy heels – you could
say we were dressed to kill. I can still remember the dress
I was wearing, black with a zip up the front, which was my
go-to pulling dress for some time.

In my drunken happiness, I started talking to a scruffy
Ed Sheeran lookalike at the bar. I asked him what he was
planning for the night and who he was out with and he
told me he 'lived in Peckham and looked after an actor
called Josh'. It was the PR guy from the other day. My
heart sunk. What the hell were the chances? I had never
been out in Peckham in my life. And there I was out with
my friends, minding my own business and that twat I'd
interviewed two days earlier was in the same bar! My face
must have said it all.

ED SHEERAN LOOKALIKE:
  Are you OK? Do you really fancy him or
  something? Most girls do.
ME: No, I only came across him the other day.
[Without any warning, this bloke barges in between us]
ED SHEERAN LOOKALIKE:
  All right, mate! Calm down! This is Josh ... sorry,
  I didn't catch your name?
  [For a split second I think I should use my
  middle name, Grace. But unfortunately, my

brain doesn't engage with my mouth quick enough]

ME: Hello, I'm Verity ... Verity Geere. You actually spoke to me down the ISDN the other day.

JOSH: Fuck me! You're the one who hadn't seen my movie and didn't have a fucking clue what you were talking about! Verity Geere who had no idea!

ME: [blushing and sweating] That's not strictly true, I had seen it. But did you realise, I had absolutely no notice and had to do the interview at the last second?

JOSH: Not my problem. Anyway, nice to meet you. And can I just say, you are hot! I didn't realise I was chatting to such a MILF! [MILF = Mother I'd Like To Fuck]

ME: A MILF?! I'm not a fucking mother!

JOSH: OK, but the rest is true! Are you single?

ME: [Coyly, going redder in the face by the second] Why, thanks! Yes, I'm single.

Josh was not only larger than life in personality, but he was incredibly gorgeous. He had a mop of thick, black hair, dark eyes, a beaming Hollywood smile, towered above me and reminded me of Keanu Reeves. I had not seen much in the trailer as he had then been dressed as a giant bird.

JOSH: Hey, we didn't get off to the best start. Can I buy you a drink?

ME: [shocked] Yes, yes that would be nice, thanks. I'll have an Aperol spritz.

JOSH: Sounds good, I'll have the same. [Shoves money in the hands of ED SHEERAN LOOKALIKE] Can you get us a couple of Aperols and whatever you want, mate?

Josh took my hand and guided me over to the edge of the dancefloor – basically a few people shuffling about on a sticky pub floor, knocking into each other. He was very smooth, but very charming, not quite the twonk I thought he was during the interview.

ME: You're much nicer in real life!

JOSH: Yeah, sorry. You probably didn't get me in my best light the other day. But I was just fed up of doing endless interviews with journalists who clearly didn't give a fuck about a movie I worked really hard on.

ME: I get that. I have to admit, I had only seen the trailer. [hide face with hand]

JOSH: I *knew* it!

ME: And the fact I had seen the trailer was only chance! I told you, I had no advance warning I was doing the interview and just did it to help out the PR guy who was ranting at me down the phone. I just can't believe out all of the places and all the people in the world, I randomly bumped into you... here in Peckham!

JOSH: Well, some might say it was fate.

ME: Yes, you could say that.
[The Killers' 'Mr Brightside' kicks in]

Man Detox

JOSH: Tuune! Do you fancy a dance?

ME: Yeah, love this track. Let's do it.

The music was blaring out so loudly, it was easier to dance and make eye contact than it was to talk. He was an amazing dancer, grabbing hold of me and spinning me around the room like a rag-doll. It was completely surreal. There I was, after a few too many Camparis, in Peckham, dancing with this comedian. For a moment I felt like I was watching my own movie play out.

JOSH: [Holding my waist with one arm and my hand with his other hand] You're a great dancer. [Leans in to kiss me]

It was as if fireworks were going off all around us, it was such a magical moment. After what seemed liked ten minutes of passionate snogging, we came up for air.

ME: I should see where my friends are.

JOSH: Sure, I'll grab our drinks off Mike.

I scurried off to the loo to check what state I was in. I had been sweating and snogging: a bad combination for a dirty pub in Peckham in the height of summer. I got to the mirrors and as predicted I looked a mess. Hair all over the place, where Josh had been combing his hands through it during our snogathon and lipstick halfway up my face. I was busy powdering my nose when Claire burst through the doors of the loos.

Fate, Full of Attraction

CLAIRE: Where the hell have you been?

ME: Oh my God, the most bizarre thing has happened. I've bumped into this comedian who I interviewed the other day. He was a total moron when I interviewed him, but he's actually really nice and *really* hot.

CLAIRE: No way, that is mad! You didn't know he was going to be here?

ME: No, of course not, he just happened to be out in Peckham too.

CLAIRE: That is fucking bonkers.

ME: I know. And what's more bonkers is I've just been snogging his face off, on the dancefloor.

CLAIRE: Fuck off! You haven't?!

ME: Yep, and he's just bought me a drink, so I'm going to pop back up to him now. I'll come and find you girls soon, if that's OK?

CLAIRE: Hell, yeah, you go guuurrl! That's awesome!

I went back to find Josh nattering in the ear of the Ed Sheeran lookalike, Mike.

JOSH: Oh, there you are! All OK with your mates?

ME: Yes, I saw my friend Claire and told her I'm on the dance floor if she needs me.

JOSH: Excellent. Let's get back to it.

He handed me my drink and we went back to him spinning me around the dance floor until we fell back into each other's arms. This time he was a lot more hands-on. I could feel his hand caress my left butt-cheek, while holding my neck and back of my hair with his other hand. It was the closest to *Dirty Dancing* I'm ever going to get.

As the night went on and the drinks kept flowing, we became more and more engrossed in each other. He even reached his hand up my thigh and ripped open the gusset of my tights, to touch my wet pussy. It was so erotic and God knows if anyone saw us, but by this stage I didn't care. I was being fingered on the dance floor of a pub in Peckham by a really good-looking comedian! This was probably never going to happen again.

And I was right. By the end of the night we parted company and failed to exchange numbers. It was completely disposable, gratuitous, raunchy fun. I probably should have been more ladylike, but I was so caught up in the obscurity of the whole thing, I just rolled with it. Instead of feeling like this is a toxic moment I needed to cleanse myself from, I actually felt like Josh was responsible for my drive to have hedonistic moments with men. I have never taken drugs, so I don't understand what people get from them. But, I remember interviewing a crystal meth addict who told me the addiction comes from desperately seeking that same high you get with the first hit. I'm not saying Josh was my man-equivalent of crystal meth, but he certainly gave me a high!

The fact that any of it happened, from the moment I answered the phone at work, to the disastrous interview, to a night out in Peckham, to the bumping into him, was all just fate. So, instead of regarding this story as toxic, I want to hold on to this as example of how some men are meant to come into your life. Reason, season or lifetime, as the saying goes. We were never going to be boyfriend and girlfriend, but it still goes down in history as one of the best nights out ever and he definitely came into my life for a reason.

ARTIST: The Killers
TITLE: 'Mr Brightside'
REASON: As last paragraph!

Chapter 8

Hot Dogs and Kittens

I was explaining to someone yesterday why I am doing a man detox and writing a book about my experience. I found myself describing it fairly succinctly.

'I feel like I am caught up in a dating revolution where technology has collided with basic animal instinct and resulted in a disposable, exhausting world of meaningless love. Where many men are looking for porno-style instant gratification in the bedroom without any romance or commitment.' Before you shout at the page, I appreciate this is not always the case. And believe me, I am doing my man detox with one hundred per cent optimism there is still a decent man out there and I just haven't met him yet. However, I have had a fair few experiences to prove my theory. Is it because of the way I have behaved myself, or have I encouraged it in my partners?

One of the pitfalls of the digital dating age is the disregard for mystery. Everyone knows when you were last online,

65

where you last 'checked in', how regularly you are online, what you were wearing last night (from the pictures you posted on your social media), the posts you have 'liked', etc. Admittedly, I could ditch social media altogether and return to the anonymity of the '90s but being permanently visible has become the way of the world and I can't fight it. As a result, many men, especially younger ones, want to see me as well as hear from me. And I don't just mean they want innocent 'Here's my new dress' pictures. I have regularly received very explicit, sometimes very unsightly photos, and pretty quickly after getting in contact with guys. And I don't get them only from the online daters.

There was one guy I worked with who took me into the 'deep depths' of his 'back catalogue'. I can't believe what he showed me were photos just for me. I'll tell you why in a moment. Chris was new to the company and needed to come to my office for training. He was only twenty-four and bounded into the office like the Andrex puppy. When I was introduced to him, I just thought, You're fit – but young. He acted like he had a lot to prove and would look over my shoulder the whole time to see if there was someone more interesting he should talking to. Later that week he came with some workmates for dinner and we got talking about our first jobs.

I regaled everyone with a story about working in a Mexican restaurant as a teenager. It was a great job with great banter, running around a bustling restaurant, juggling the hot fajita plates with bottles of *cerveza* (sometimes swigging one). I was pretty good at chatting with – and chatting up – customers, but not very good at the actual job. The chefs used to get really annoyed with me for coming away with the biggest tips while doing the least table-clearing and washing-up. One day – bear in mind I was a *very* naive fifteen-year-old – a chef in the kitchen shouted '*Verity*, shift your clit!' Stony-faced, I replied, 'OK'. I knew it must have meant 'speed up' but I genuinely didn't understand what he meant.

I told this story to the guys over dinner, laughing about the fact I was completely unaware of the definition of 'clit'. It shows you how far we've come in the workplace, as that comment would be totally unacceptable now but was just passed off as banter in 1994. What I failed to notice was how funny Chris thought this was. The next day at work he would whisper at any given opportunity, 'Shift your clit,' giving himself the biggest laugh in the process and leaving me smiling through gritted teeth and scarlet.

He started to get his confident, twenty-four-year-old feet firmly under the desk at work and when we met in an empty corridor, he made a point of holding the door to the studio open for me. As I went through it he whispered, 'How do feel about me *actually* shifting your clit?'

I laughed it off but in my head I was thinking Whaaat...? and swaggered back to my desk with the knowledge that a hot younger man had just come on to thirty-seven-year-old me.

The thing was, this ribald comment sowed a seed in my head. The cheeky, way-too-young-for-me, tall, virile, gorgeous new boy had just made sexual advances towards *me*! Chunky-thighed, slightly wrinkly, been-around-the-block, saggy-boobed me?! Initially I was dubious and thought, Why are you picking me? I'm not senior enough to help you further your career. I'm not as pretty as Jess from finance. I live too far from you to take this any further. I was totally flummoxed but flattered at the same time.

I was doing a story about how to tone your obliques, a very attractive area on a man's body and what my gay friend lovingly calls 'cum gutters'. I did a short survey around the office to see if I could find the best ones by getting the men to show me. I knew at the back of my mind that young, toned newbie Chris would obviously have amazing cum gutters, but what he didn't realise was I had filmed this gem of a moment. And sent the video to the group I had been out for dinner with. He quickly fired me a private message on Facebook and a long message conversation ensued while we were both out on a Friday night:

CHRIS: You filmed me!!!!!! Hahahaha I thought it was a picture x

ME: Are you cross?! It's AMAZING! I only sent it to our dinner group.

CHRIS: Not at all!!! Haha amused and flattered ;o x

ME: I watched it this afternoon. Actually didn't realise I'd videoed it either.

CHRIS: That old chestnut. I'll work on it so when I see you in a few months it looks better!! X

ME: Tell me about it. I'm using the summer to detox, get brown and toned... you won't recognise me x

CHRIS: Seriously I'm gunna do it! Already can't wait!! And I'll improve the cum gutters especially for you x

ME: Lol!! No improvement necessary! Love that

you're adopting all my rude sayings. Don't be spoiling other colleagues with those CGs x

CHRIS: Hahaha again very kind of you. I'm sure there is much I could be taught x

ME: I would show you such a good time! X

CHRIS: I look forward to it! ;o x

ME: Feel naughty flirting with you

CHRIS: Don't :) I like it ;o x

ME: OK, well I'm in a very naughty mood...

CHRIS: Haha ;o love that!! Sounds good to me ;o x

ME: My friend who turns 37 today is currently pulling a 21 year old. Who cares about age?! Xx

CHRIS: Haha love that !!!

ME: Sharing an air bnb with my friend, SO earplugs at the ready xx

CHRIS: Haha!! Oh no!! You should have pulled as well so you can beat them to it xx

ME: How about you?? Any action?! xx

CHRIS: Nope not so far, haha!! Maybe I should improve the cum gutters haha xx

ME: Haha! I'm pretty selective and I'm sure you are too. Not many people have a video of your cum gutters xx

CHRIS: Nobody has ... you are the one and only and it's not a bad thing to be selective xx

ME: Had enough playing gooseberry so now back at bnb. At least I have some video footage to keep me entertained xx

CHRIS: Haha!!! I mean as far as it goes there is probably better videos to have. I think I'll reserve those for an in person meeting xx

ME: I'll have to return the favour.

CHRIS: I mean... I welcome any female equivalent you have of my cum gutters xx

ME: Valley of sin? X

CHRIS: Now that sounds like something I wanna see xx

ME: Ha! The saying is 'flooding the valley of sin'...

CHRIS: Well now flooding the valley of sin sounds like something I definitely want to do, why are you so far away :(xx

ME: Ha! I know, so horny right now as well xx

CHRIS: Don't say that! Makes it worse! I can't even send you a pic... I'm still out!! Xx

ME: That's what afternoons are for when you're a breakfast presenter xx

CHRIS: I like the sound of that!! Did you say you were going to pop along to that little get together on Friday? Because if so I'll pop down after the show ;o xx

ME: Pop into mine en route if you fancy? ;o xx

CHRIS: Now that is an offer I couldn't refuse ;o that's my Friday sorted... something to look forward too xx

ME: Awesome! Looking forward too xx

A few hours later...

ME: [drunk at the end of the night] SENT PIC [cleavage with bra on]

CHRIS: SENT PIC [of giant erection]

ME: I knew you wouldn't disappoint... look at that hidden weaponry!!

CHRIS: I mean... when you sent that picture last night, I had the lads crashing on my floor so there wasn't much I could do... but I wanted to repay the favour ;o xx

ME: Lol! As long that pic remained private!! Can I admit, I had already 'used' your video for my pleasure on Friday xx

CHRIS: You did? Oooh sounds fun xx

ME: That pic has superseded the cum gutters vid xx

The messages started off fairly innocent, but soon developed into very flirty exchanges. The pics started off fairly bland and faceless. But they soon escalated and I was constantly checking my phone for my next emoji-filled, sexually explicit instalment. The problem with this appetite for sexting and images is the constant use of imagination needed to keep them interesting. Chris had introduced me to a very risqué world of teasing each other with pics, which obviously built up the sexual tension between us before the inevitable happened. Those knowing glances across the office from him, after he had already seen my underwear that day, were nothing short of exhilarating. I don't normally write a diary but I've taken notes on my phone:

28 July

I am a thirty-seven-year-old woman about to sleep with a younger man (twenty-four) and instead of treating it like a serious proposition that he's going to fall for me, I'm treating it as an experiment. He is a new colleague at work and out of all the women, many of whom are younger, he has chosen me to flirt with.

I just don't get it! However, the intrigue is too much to bear, so I'm just going along with it. We started by flirting in the office, which then transferred to messages and it rapidly got dirty. Part of me likes the thrill that he's forbidden fruit (don't poke the payroll) and part of me is thrilled he's interested at all. Friends I've spoken to tell me it's the lure of 'an older woman'. He's not really my type; skinny, fair. But I just *know* he's going to be energetic and fun in the bedroom. I'm a bit scared I won't keep up, but I'm keen to find out.

We eventually did the deed before a work night out. I spent hours getting ready, making sure I was manicured in every department and smelling amazing. By the time he arrived I had almost already orgasmed. The thought of this gorgeous, younger man coming to satisfy me was almost too much to bear. By the time he got to my house we only had an hour or so to play. I offered him a drink and he said, 'I need to make the most of you.'

He started kissing me so intensely that the back of my head was pressing into the corner of the sofa. He manhandled my breasts and started to creep his hand up to my wet pussy. He was not better than any other man, but he was twenty-four-year-old Chris and he could be with any woman he wanted – but he had chosen me. I suggested that we go to the bedroom as it was getting too awkward on the sofa. I wanted to jump his bones!

Once we got to my bedroom, there were no sexy stripteases: we both just took our clothes off. I slid my black dress over my head and was left with my underwear, and he took off his jeans and shirt. I pulled aside my thong to slip on top of his rock-hard cock and I made sure I was satisfied. He moved me around to a few positions, but it didn't last very long. I was fine with that, though, as the tension ahead of our liaison had been exhausting! After being ravaged, we brushed ourselves off to look less like we'd been having sex before we headed to the work drinks.

For such a young guy he had a great sporty car and the hard acceleration pumped through me, giving another rush of adrenaline, like I was a teenager all over again. At the drinks, the sexual tension between us was electric. I could still feel his cum seeping into my knickers all through the evening. And he did a good job of giving me knowing glances and ignoring me at the same time so no one suspected anything. He didn't really know how to behave with me, but did a good job of making sure I didn't feel fucked over.

At the end of the night he offered me a lift. As we drove he placed his left hand on my thigh, and I reached over to his 'gear stick' and felt that he was hard again. I suggested that we 'do something about that'. So we returned back to my flat for round two. Not exactly the sex of my life but he was very confident, and on both occasions it was all over and done with pretty quickly.

After this night out, the naughtiness was kept alive for a few weeks with filthy messages, photos and eventually videos. I wrote more notes:

16 September
So, here I am after sleeping with Chris and I have thought about little else. We slept together weeks ago and I have heard from him fairly regularly. It

started off pretty intense and then he seemed to lose interest. We sent each other pictures and videos of us pleasuring ourselves. Only so many videos of his hard cock exploding with hot semen I need to see. Bit of torment really! But it has been a genuinely exciting/turn on/flattering experience. Even though I might see him again, I know I need to be kind to myself and stop messing about with men (boys) who only want me for one thing. Chris is never going to turn around and say, 'Hey, let's make a go of this.' He's thirteen years younger than me! He turned twenty-five at the weekend and it got me thinking, What was I doing at twenty-five? The fact that I could barely remember said it all. I am constantly surrounded by gorgeous families with little ones, which is a constant reminder that I want that too. Something Chris is not going to be ready for, for many years to come. I am, after all, just an 'older bird trophy'! Who knows what's round the corner but if anything, he's given me a boost and made me realise I've still got it. *Even* a twenty-five-year-old wants to fuck me!

It was a steamy hot summer and the hormones were raging for both of us. It was so exhilarating. Waking up in the morning to see pictures of his hard cock with a message saying, 'Thinking of you this morning'. I would check my phone incessantly throughout the day for more filthy descriptions of what he wanted to do to me to keep me going until the evening when I was the most uninhibited I have ever been with a man. Looking back, I genuinely believe the thought of sex and the pictorial teases were better than the reality. Eventually the messages tailed off and after a few weeks of him off-grid I sent a message to test the water:

ME: I had a dream about sucking you last night. [no response]

ME: Am I embarrassing myself?!

CHRIS: Don't worry you aren't embarrassing yourself, I just don't know what to say!

ME: No need to say anything!! You've obviously had a change of heart about us sending each other dirty messages. You just popped into my head. God knows why I'm dreaming about you after all this time!

CHRIS: I think I just don't wanna mess up how well we get along and its a difficult one with work and stuff and I do feel bad. I hope we can still get along as friends cos I would like that.

ME: Oh God, no change here! We had our fun! I'm seeing a guy, so shouldn't be dreaming about you!!!

CHRIS: So worried I'd pissed you off!! Don't want this to be the case!

ME: No way!! Why would you piss me off?! Honestly, you treated me better than some men!!

CHRIS: But still! Ha. Glad you are seeing someone though! Dates also going good my end!

Fortunately, it all ended mutually after a few months. I understood that he had got what he wanted from me and vice versa. It wasn't going anywhere between us. It was never going to be something meaningful as there was too much of an age gap. Essentially, I had got carried away with the flattery of a much younger man. As far as the world of sexting was concerned, I can't deny it was bawdy and to some extent I encouraged him, but I did wonder if he was sending pics from an archive. I think men his age are so used to producing 'dick pics' they just forward you ones they've sent to other women: how kind! I also think that men of his generation have come to expect that kind of interaction, as messages are laborious to type and not as satisfying or exciting. I don't know whether this is as a direct result of the booming online porn industry or whether kids these days (I sound so old) have just grown up with smart phones and it has become completely the norm.

I admit I was swept up in the moment and, yes, I do regret it, but all of the footage I took was anonymous and I did trust him not to send it on to anyone. In answer to my own question about whether I could have done anything differently – well, I could have ignored his advances in the first place, but it was fun. But I've definitely now come to the conclusion that these pics titillate me about as much as photos of hot dogs and kittens!

ARTIST: Sam Smith
TITLE: 'Too Good at Goodbyes'
REASON: The lyrics about not standing a chance – it certainly was both true and sad.

Chapter 9

Heartbreak Test

It's Day 16 of the man detox and I've had my biggest test yet.

I started this experiment for a number of reasons, but ultimately I'm trying to self-help and mend my broken heart over Ben. I am hurting and this is because I want to be with this man who doesn't want to be with me. It's hard to even type this. It's funny how heartbreak can be felt physically. I've had heartache a fair few times and it really can make your chest feel like it's burning and throbbing. My mind plays tricks on me, making me think about Ben and I feel an instant nausea and adrenaline.

I have even stood in front of the mirror and given the speech I want to give him. I am brave in front of the mirror, I guess, because I know he will never hear it. It goes along the lines of:

I want to tell you everything about how I am feeling right now. I love you and I want to know why I am not good enough for you. One day you were there, the next day you weren't. You told me how beautiful I am. To me, you are the most gorgeous person I've ever met, inside and out. You told me we had a great connection. You wanted to tell me everything about your day and your life. I would do anything for you. You wanted to share your life with me for that moment in time, so why can't it be like that forever? Why were you able to show me so much love and attention and then ruthlessly cut me off? Am I not pretty enough for you? Am I not thin enough for you? You told me I turned you on. And on every level we were right for each other. We were having such a good time, laughing so much, so at ease with one another. Why can't we keep having a good time?'

There are so many love songs along these lines too. So many songs about being torn apart from someone. Songs about being in love one minute and asking 'Why am I not enough?' the next. I torment myself in front of the mirror and mull over these thoughts in the middle of the night when I lose all perspective in the darkness. With previous episodes of heartbreak, I've wanted to be sick. Not wanted to eat for days. I've even punched a wall. When I split up with my first long-term boyfriend (of four years) I was twenty-three and sent eighty texts in one day. Needless to say, this did not win him back.

My course of action these days is to do nothing. The benefit of getting older is that experience leads to wisdom. I have learnt to deal with these inner battles, on my own and by discussing them with anyone except the person concerned. I started writing about my current heartbreak with Ben the other day. Since then, I have been asked by numerous close friends and family, 'How are you feeling about Ben?' The questioners include my great aunt who lives near Ben and who I visited regularly when I saw him. At the grand old age of eighty-three, Auntie offers me a lot of her wisdom.

Her first words this week were, 'Have you heard from that horrible man?' I was quick to defend him, saying he's not horrible – it's just not good timing. She was quick to retort, 'No, Verity, you are a wonderful lady, who deserves nothing but the best and I don't understand why Ben is not fighting to keep you.' This was very sweet of her and although she is biased, it was ringing in my ears for a while. Which was fortuitous, as I had my biggest test yet today, a heartbreak test, a message from Ben. It simply said: 'Hey, Just a hello :) hope you're doing well and all is good Xx'.

I instantly felt sick. Just that image of a WhatsApp message arriving with his name on it was enough to send a lightning bolt through my heart. Over the last couple of weeks, I have felt like the deep wound of my broken heart was starting to scab over. Unfortunately, this message from Ben caught that scab and ripped it off. In the few weeks since I heard from him, I've felt more and more like he doesn't care, he's not that interested, and maybe he's moved on to someone else. But this message made me think he *does* care, a little. My immediate impulse was to reply, in my usual bright-and-breezy style, acting like everything was fine. But my self-imposed NOmenBER rules mean I can't reply. This has taken every fibre of my being.

I don't know what the future holds. But as I regularly point out to a radio colleague, Adam, this is the case for everything, anywhere and any time. You often hear a reporter finish with the words, 'The future remains to be seen' or 'Only time will tell' or 'What's around the corner is anyone's guess.' No shit, Sherlock! Such lazy journalism. Adam and I now always send each other a WhatsApp message when we spot those clichés used as a pay-off.

However, these words are all too true for Ben and me, as the future *does* remain to be seen. I must remember how far I've come, even in sixteen days. I've been telling myself I mustn't take the crumbs. I have started to repair, by letting out the raw emotions. I have no idea if this man detox is going to work but I'm proud of myself for trying. One thing's for sure: offloading all my thoughts is definitely making me feel better, so thanks for joining me on my journey.

ARTIST: Rebecca Ferguson
TITLE: 'Bones'
REASON: The lyrics sum it all up.

Chapter 10

Play-Doh

Today I'm asking for forgiveness, as I've realised there may have been some men who need a detox from me after the way I treated them.

I have been taking advantage of having more time on my hands. (It's amazing how many hours I have lost swiping left and right.) In order to properly detox, I have been 'cleansing' my physical environment as well as my mind. I have cleared out three sack-loads of clothes, shoes and general rubbish and I've ruthlessly disposed of a lot of memorabilia. I'm not particularly nostalgic but I have held on to the odd keepsake, including an invitation to a fortieth birthday.

I went to the party with a guy I dated a couple of years ago but then kind of forgot about. The party was in January when I was starting yet another new year single. I came up with the idea of scanning my Facebook friends to double-check if there were any acquaintances I had connected with who might be a potential date. There he was. A chap called Andrew I had met on a couple of occasions and I remembered how lovely he was. I didn't know him well, but we had several work friends in common. I messaged to suggest we met up to discuss our work, as a kind of networking lunch. We met at a high-end cafe in Soho and, when I first saw him, I was surprised by how handsome he looked. After catching up on work-related chat, we soon got on to the subject of dating. He too was struggling to meet a like-minded person.

From that lunch we went on a few dates and after a few weeks had our first snog. I remember thinking to myself that his kiss was so enthusiastic it was like it was his first-ever, even though he was mid-thirties. His technique involved proper plunger-like suction, with washing machine-style tongue action and hands like Mr Tickle, all over my boobs, bum, waist, inner thigh, neck, hair... you name it. There's nothing like a sensual and seductive kiss, and this was nothing like a sensual and seductive kiss. He ravaged me! I just humoured him and put his overzealous kissing down to a recent lack of action.

I was working away from home a fair bit and was staying in hotels. Andrew lived with his mum, so I suggested he came to stay with me for the night. He brought along a bag with neatly packed clothes – and a couple of dog-eared teddies! When I asked, he just said, 'Oh, yeah, Noodle and Scratcher come everywhere with me. I've had them since I was a kid.' I wanted to laugh so badly but at the same time he was so sweet I didn't want to be offensive.

I was staying in a fairly dingy hotel and it was nice have him to cuddle up to. This soon progressed into some more (overzealous) kissing. And then some heavy petting (like the behaviour banned in swimming pools in the '80s), although this was more like heavy-handed petting. His attempts to jam his fingers inside me fell far short of the sensual stimulation I was after. It seemed the kissing had been a fairly accurate trailer for the film. We attempted to have sex, but again, his 'enthusiasm' meant his stamina was short-lived. The experience was akin to stuffing Play-Doh in a pillar box. Soon after the deed was done, he told me he needed to 'take a minute'.

He opened his perfectly packed overnight bag and took out a Bible. This fell open on a specific page and he knelt down at the end of the bed, in front of his Bible, and started praying. I assumed he was praying for forgiveness for the act he had just committed. Not knowing where to look, I just scrolled through my phone until he finished pleading to God. I knew he was religious, but I didn't know *how* religious. But the thing was, Andrew was a really lovely, kind guy. Exactly what I thought I wanted, but this had slightly thrown me.

I decided to give him the benefit of the doubt as far as his terrible bedroom skills went. We continued to see each other for a few weeks but each time we slept together it was the same. I thought I could show him how to improve his performance, but there was no increase in stamina or decrease in manhandling, despite my comments such as, 'Ouch! Try being a little less rigorous.' His commitment to his faith wasn't a problem, although I could tell he was riddled with guilt.

I was surprised when he suggested a sleepover at his mum's house. Cathy was a very sweet lady but their house, a modest semi, was absolutely rammed with clutter going back forty years and thick with as many years' worth of dust. Andrew was obsessed with buses. With him being her favourite son, Cathy had dedicated the lounge to Andrew's bus collection. Anything bus-related you care to mention adorned that front room. Model buses from bygone years through to the modern age, bus stop signs, bus maps, a bus conductor hat... I had never seen anything like it.

Cathy was very welcoming, acting like Andrew had never met a woman before. As soon as he was out of earshot, she held my hand (eyes welling up) and told me how thrilled she was God had finally found him 'a good lady'. She could not do enough, offering me tea, coffee, biscuits, hot food, cold food. She asked if I was warm enough, comfortable enough and allowed me to sit in the 'best seat' in the lounge. As a 'special treat' she was going to let Andrew and I stay in her bed. This was very kind, but I did feel pretty uncomfortable about the idea.

Before we got to his mother's bed, we went to the fortieth birthday party I mentioned earlier. It was for Andrew's best friend Laura. It was a lavish event in central London and again, Laura and all the party guests were thrilled (verging on shocked) that I was Andrew's new girlfriend. To be honest, I was pretty shocked too, as we hadn't really discussed it, but I went along for the night, as he went around introducing me to everyone as 'my girlfriend, Verity'. It turned out that all of these friends were from Andrew's church. They were very sweet, although all of them quizzed me, 'How's it going with Andrew?' like it was the biggest-breaking news story they'd heard all year.

Back at Cathy's, after the party, we did indeed turn in

for the night in his mother's bed. It was weird but it would have offended her if we hadn't after she had tidied up and changed the sheets. As we'd had a few cocktails at the party we were quite frisky and one thing led to another. I was determined to enjoy myself. I went on top, as I found this usually guaranteed satisfaction for me. The problem was, there appeared to be a terrible rattle every time we were grinding against each other. I was so worried about us waking up his brother in the next room or his mum who was the other side of the hallway. There was in any case a complete lack of rhythm and synchronisation with our two bodies, and this strange rattle only added to the dissatisfaction. When the light went on, I realised the noise was made by Cathy's rosary beads smacking against the bedpost. This was beyond excruciating. Not only was I having sex in my 'boyfriend's' mother's bed, I was being audibly reminded this activity was against Andrew's and/or his family's religious beliefs.

The next morning, I couldn't get out of the house fast enough. I turned down Cathy's offer of a full English at the specially laid dining room table and I drove away from his house filled with disgust for myself. After discussing the situation with my best friend, I decided it wasn't really my fault: we were just too different. Later that day, I – very cowardly – sent him a text message: 'Hey Lovely, I wish I didn't feel like this but I do... I wanted to explain myself so decided to write it down... I'm just not feeling it between us. That's not fair on you. You are a wonderful person but you deserve someone who feels the same about you as you do about them. Rather than stringing it out any longer to see what happens, it's better that I'm just honest. I'm so sorry and hope you will forgive me. Writing this is a really hard thing to do but I needed to tell you how I feel sooner rather than later, Vxx'

Oh my God (sorry God) I was such a cow. I didn't even call him. I dumped him by text!!! But essentially I knew I needed a quick exit, without seeing him. And he didn't take it well. After a few days he replied, 'Hey, hope you're having a good day. It's taken me a couple of days to digest your message. Totally unexpected to be honest. Didn't see that coming. Thought the feelings were mutual. By text as well. Would have been good to have a chat on the phone at least. Regardless, respect your decision. If you're not feeling it then you have to be honest. Enjoyed your company and your time. It was fun while it lasted. Hope you find what you desire. That's important.'

A few more days passed and then he got back in touch: 'It would be great if we can talk. Not really OK to be honest. Very confused. We don't talk as much as we used to. It's gone silent. I'm not angry with you if you think I am – not at all. Be honest and tell me if there was a specific reason. Feel as if I've done something wrong. It's cut me up rather badly. Haven't been able to sleep or function properly. Feel as you've cut me off x'

This was one of many, many messages he sent, asking me questions and begging me back. In the end I had to tell him to leave me alone. He was such a sweet guy, but he hadn't got a clue what he was doing in the bedroom. I know this is not the be-all and end-all, but it's very important to me. More importantly, I didn't want to be made to feel guilty for having (rubbish) sex – his prayers at the end of each session shouldn't have been for forgiveness but for sexual improvement. But when I think about some of the 'Slumberland test-pilots' I've been with, maybe I should have held on tightly to a good guy who only wanted to love me. He wouldn't have cheated or constantly made me feel like there was someone better over my shoulder.

This is why, as part of today's detox, I'm asking the universe for forgiveness. I was so mean to Andrew. I just dumped him from a great height by text, when he thought everything was going really well. I didn't have the nerve to tell him the truth. And until now, I had just parked that short-lived relationship in a memory box and tried to forget about him. To this day, I don't know if he was a virgin, but I am sorry I effectively ghosted him because of his Play-Doh phallus.

ARTIST: Snakehips featuring Zayn
TITLE: 'Cruel'
REASON: This song came out around the time I was cruel to Andrew.

Chapter 11

Digging Deep

Day 19 and even though this detox is a mental exercise, I genuinely feel I am ridding my body of physical toxins too.

Today, I had a banging headache and woke up with spots, which is quite unusual for me. It amazes me how my body seems to understand I am making changes, but it is off-loading a lot of crap and my skin is reflecting that. I went to meet some girlfriends for breakfast and, without meaning to, I burst into tears the minute I saw them. I used the excuse that I was stressed out by traffic, finding a parking space and getting to them on time. But they knew I was bottling up some emotions.

I appreciate that letting out a few tears hardly flushes away twenty-five years' of emotional man-toxins, but as my girlfriends told me, 'It's good to cry.' Not only am I still feeling the burn from not replying to Ben's message but I've realised I'm also letting out other frustrations. I'm constantly asking myself, Why am I not good enough? What could I do differently to be the one men want? Do I need to be thinner or prettier? Should I join the tennis club? Should I hang out in the real ale pubs where men go? These kind of questions have never really gone away. Since I can remember, I have not felt good enough and have been grateful for any attention I could get.

I was fourteen when got my first ever 'boyfriend'. I was fresh from an all-girls convent school and the excitement of having boys in my new class was almost too much to bear and a constant distraction. Milo Hamilton was thirteen, as his birthday was in August and mine was in September. We were in the same school year, but there was almost a year between us, which was huge at that age. He was that boy who was excellent at every subject that I was terrible at, so I thought he might be able to help me with my homework. He looked exactly like Penfold the hamster sidekick from *Danger Mouse*, with thick, black-rimmed glasses and a chubby face. He also had floppy curtains of hair and was the same height as me. He was a total geek, but I liked him.

I didn't really understand what fancying meant or what 'going out with someone' was, but I knew it was akin to having a boyfriend and that was all I'd ever wanted. All my friends had been 'going out with' boyfriends for ages and I felt like the ugly one left out of the sports team. Ours was an idyllic school in a small Hampshire town where the worst thing that ever happened was a few smokers getting caught behind the bushes and someone spray-creaming a knob on the bus shelter (not even using proper graffiti paint).

Digging Deep

As soon as I was passed a scribbled note via my friend Kate, 'Will you go out with me? From Milo Hamilton', I promptly replied underneath with, 'Yes'. I claimed I had fancied him for ages, but the truth was I just wanted someone rather than no one. It was such a tricky time, with hormones flying all over the place, love notes being passed from person to person during class. But it was innocent and I'm so glad I had my childhood before mobile phones. I would race home from school and spend hours on the phone to Kate and Mary, my best friends. I had spent all day at school with them, but we still had so much endless nonsense to discuss all evening on the landline, dragged from the hallway into the privacy of the downstairs loo. Kate couldn't wait to congratulate me on my new boyfriend. But I admitted to her immediately that I had my doubts.

ME: What if I have to kiss him?

KATE: Ew, you might have to.

ME: I only said 'Yes' to him because I want a
        boyfriend. Is that really bad?

KATE: No, I get that. And he's sweet.

ME: But I just want to go out with him. You know,
        go out to the cinema and stuff.

KATE: Well, that's cool. Why don't we? We could go on
        a double-date with you, me, Chris and Milo.

Kate was so much prettier than me and had been with Chris for a few months, an eternity in those days. She had luscious, dark-brown hair, long, dark eyelashes, green eyes, a perfect size 8 figure and big boobs. Every teenage boy's dream. I had the massive boobs, but also terrible, frizzy mousy hair constantly scraped back in a bun, and pale skin. I went from kids clothes to a size 14 around the age of ten, and have pretty much remained there ever since. I hadn't started exploring the makeup aisles of Boots yet, but had very natural fair eyelashes and a plain complexion, and I wore a lot of turtleneck sweaters and baggy jeans.

I had been pining over the hottest boy in our year for months, but he chose Kate and despite my inner heartbreak I just had to be happy for her. There was lots of swapping of partners going on, even back then. Certain girls in my year would date all of the hot boys, just because they could. There were rumours that Kelly Frost, who was really cool and smoked and everything, had already slept with three boys, a massive talking point. But I knew I didn't want anything 'serious' – I just wanted to hold hands with Milo and go to the village stream with him, where it was quiet and romantic. Instead, Milo invited me to his house for tea, so we could do our homework together.

I was so excited but at the same time terrified that he might lunge at me and expect me to kiss him, like they did in the soaps. We'd be tilting our heads from side to side, tongues slobbering around all over the place like Scott and Charlene on *Neighbours*. I had never done this and didn't really want to either – Milo was very funny and constantly made me giggle, but he didn't really give me the tickle in my tummy that I got from other boys. We just did our homework as planned, watched TV and fortunately there was no leaning over me with his lips pursed expectantly. I mentioned to him that Kate and I had discussed going to the cinema and he said he was keen, so we spoke to our parents and made arrangements for one set of parents to drive us there and one to pick us up.

The next day in food technology – a class that still haunts me to this day – we were waiting for Miss Baker to come in when Kelly Frost shouted from across the other side of the classroom, 'Oi, Verity, are you going out with that fucking dweeb, Milo Hamilton?' I was absolutely mortified. A load of people around the class giggled and I went bright red, trying to ignore her. Moments later she continued at the same volume, ''Cos if you are, you can do a lot better than him!' I have never forgotten that, because I knew what she meant. I felt defensive of him in some respects, but I didn't think anyone cool would ever want to go out with me. He was better than no one.

We did go to the cinema with Kate and Chris, but Kelly Frost's comments played on my mind all evening. As soon as I got home with Kate, I plucked up the courage to phone Milo and tell him it was over. He didn't seem overly fussed I was dumping him, but I remember feeling a huge sense of relief. I had felt so much pressure to be someone's girlfriend, even at that young age. I feel mixed emotions as I write about this. I can laugh at the whole scenario but it also makes me feel sad for my fourteen-year-old self. My insecurities are deep-rooted and my insistence on being 'grateful' for any male attention has always been a poisoned chalice. I am so grateful for having such a charmed upbringing, going to a lovely school and living in a nice area. It has enabled me to be the confident, bubbly person I am. However, I have always put boys on a pedestal and been a bit too keen to massage their ego by saying 'Yes' to them, rather than 'Yes' to me and what I want.

It's been hard digging deep and admitting to myself that this pattern of behaviour started from the word go with Milo Hamilton. I just 'went out' with him because he asked me. It's a coincidence that today has been an emotional one. But as the girls said, it's OK to cry – in fact, cry like a waterfall if necessary.

ARTIST: Green Day
TITLE: 'Basket Case'
REASON: This song is synonymous with my school days.

Chapter 12

Girls Compete, Women Empower Each Other

A lot of the time I hate self-help slogans, but I saw one today – 'Girls compete, women empower each other' – and it resonated with me. Sometimes good things come from dire situations, when you least expect them. Girlfriends are really important to me, as I am fiercely close to mine and they are effectively my chosen sisters. This week I had an exciting brunch with a girl I met in very unlikely circumstances.

I don't like to tar all online dates with the same brush, but a few of the men I've met have not quite been who they proclaimed to be. It's way too easy to pretend to be someone you're not online. And that's why I try to insist on meeting men pretty soon after first connecting.

Dan was a guy I met on Bumble. He was not particularly my type – posh, fairly shy, tubby and short – but he was a well turned-out businessman and very charming. He started messaging me immediately after we exchanged numbers, but using texts as opposed to WhatsApp, although I could see he had a WhatsApp profile (which is pretty key to this story). We met for dinner a couple of times, which was very civilised, but over the course of six weeks we didn't even kiss. It might seem pretty normal not to kiss so early on, but this was in the context of him being in contact with me morning, noon and night with messages about his day. He showed a helluva lot of interest for someone who didn't want to try to kiss me.

Over Easter he had sent me a photo of the most delicious-looking chocolate pudding, with a Creme Egg oozing out of it. Without mentioning Dan, I tweeted the photo of this pudding. A few days later I received a direct message on Twitter: 'Hi Verity, there is no reason why you would know me, but we seem to have a mutual contact, Dan, who until yesterday, I had been in a seven-month, romantic/sexual relationship with. I found out from messages that not only had he been on dates with you (maybe more, I don't know), even sent you a picture of the Creme Egg dessert we had made together, he had also been seeing someone else (kissed her) and messaging another. He insists that nothing happened and has given his excuses as to why, and although I'm trying to work out what all this means, and not sure I ever will, from woman to woman, I wanted to hear it from you... an honest account. Women are always quick to blame the other, but I believe this dishonesty and incomplete madness is all him. I'm sorry for involving you like this... God only knows what he would say if he knew I had messaged you, but I just need to know what happened, so that I can work this out and move on. Thank you, Nicola x.'

This was nothing other than a moment when I felt as if I'd been punched in the stomach. It was 6 a.m., just before I went on air to do my radio show, and I felt sick that I had been unknowingly dating somebody else's guy and hurt the other woman in this way. I wasn't even that bothered about Dan, but I had wasted six weeks speaking to someone who wasn't who he said he was. I immediately replied, 'Hi there, I totally understand why you would contact me in these difficult circumstances. I can confirm we only went on two dates and nothing happened. He messaged me most days for the six weeks that we knew each other, updating me on his work, tennis, family life. But on the two occasions I met him he didn't kiss me. I found the whole thing a bit odd, to be honest. I met him on Bumble and he told me he was looking for a partner with chemistry who was also his best friend. From what I could tell, his ex-wife had model looks but essentially used him for a passport. And he very much made me feel like I didn't live up to those model looks! Therefore, I realised after just two dates he was too shallow for me. I'm so, so sorry if you have been let down by him, but you messaging me today has very much confirmed my suspicions, he is not the man he professes to be. I hope you can work things out. I for one will never be having anything to do with him again, Vx.'

Nicola: 'Hello Verity, thank you for replying so quickly. I'm also starting to realise that he isn't the man he claims to be. We spent every weekend together, have recently been on holiday, I've spent time with his family and friends, and yet it seems I don't really know the man! He has also made me feel that I'm not good enough... He claims everything is there but it's missing something. I don't think anyone or anything will be good enough for him. He has actually been married twice... not that I knew that one of them had model looks, but again, it probably had nothing to do with them and was his poor behaviour that probably brought things to an end. He has asked me to forgive him whilst *he* goes away and thinks if what we have is enough... In fact, what we had isn't enough for me! I also will never be having anything to do with him! Thanks again and good luck finding the "one". Although I'm not quite sure they exist! Nicola x.'

Me: 'You're so welcome. Like you say, us women have to stick together! I can't believe he thinks this behaviour is acceptable. Married twice?! Wow, that says a lot. Anyway, if you can find the strength to walk away, you will definitely be better off. I'm going on a new date tonight... Dan who?! Vx.'

Nicola: 'Great. Well, let's hope this is the man of your dreams! I am walking away, but it's a little raw at the moment. It was only last week I was the supportive girlfriend on the one-year anniversary of his father's death! He talks about this immense chemistry that he is looking for and that he apparently had with both of his wives, but I am starting to realise that he loves himself way too much! Good luck for tonight. Us girls do need to stick together, I'm all for that! Nicola x.'

Me: 'I'm sure you are raw, what he's done is very hurtful. Just be kind to yourself and surround yourself with nice, supportive and fun people. You sound like a great girl, waaay too good for him! Vx.'

Nicola: 'Thanks, Verity! One thing he doesn't know, I've

actually kept it from him, is that I'm a psychic medium. Unfortunately never get anything for myself, but that's how I caught him out! I'm seriously done with him. I just need to process it. He has high thoughts of himself and God knows why! So very strange... he will end up a lonely old man! X.'

Me: 'I thought that! I'm not being funny, but I am capable of dating much better looking/successful men, but he seems to have an unsubstantiated high opinion of himself. That's so fascinating you are a psychic medium! I'm so drawn to spiritual people like you. You'll have to tell me if you get any readings from me! Is that what you do for a living? Vx.'

Nicola: 'No, I work in finance. I just do the medium/ spirit things for fun. Have a lot of clients and it's always fun to do a reading. If you ever fancy one, let me know – would be happy to. And thanks for your messages, I feel so much better than yesterday xx.'

Me: 'Amazing! I might take you up on that, as a friend of mine and I have been saying we want to go for readings! I used to live in LA and people go to see psychic mediums as much as they go to the doc over there! Vx,'

A few hours later, Nicola wrote again. 'By the way, my friends think Dan was a con-man. He moved out of his apartment in August and his furniture was for sale on Facebook. Also resigned as director of two of his supposed companies.'

Me: 'Wow! How did you hear all this? Prob on a "wanted" list somewhere?!'

Nicola: 'Yes, I can't believe I wasted seven months on him. He did keep going on about how he needed some investment. I just ignored it, but looking back now it was a bit odd. I did go to his apartment in Spain. That was when he started messaging you, I think. And the others!'

Me: 'Cracks me up to be honest, as I was taking a punt on a "geeky chubby one" with him!'

Nicola: 'A cheeky, chubby con-man.'

Dan had always made sure he texted me instead of WhatsApping, presumably to ensure he wasn't seen online chatting to me. It seems he was a businessman but a terrible one, whose 'property empire' comprised a one-bedroom flat that he needed to sell, and his one failed marriage turned out to be *two* failed marriages. 'His' house in Spain, which he had showed me pictures of, belonged to his father. But worst of all, he had a girlfriend *and* he was shagging about, getting his end away wherever he could. After much deliberation I decided to write to him and told him what I thought of him: 'Today I have received a message from a heartbroken woman, who is apparently your girlfriend. When I start dating someone, I like to trust they are single and available, but it turns out this was not the case. I thought this woman was very brave to message me and ask what had happened between us. Who do you think you are? Spinning a web of lies and hurting people along the way? Needless to say, I don't want anything to do with you ever again.'

I didn't hear from him, but I just needed to tell him what a two-timing bastard I thought he was. I also posted about this on Facebook and was overwhelmed with responses from people, agreeing that us women have to stick together in situations like this. He was not a nice person and neither Nicola nor I deserved to be treated like that.

Girls Compete, Women Empower Each Other

The silver lining to this story is that Nicola and I are now friends. This week I went for brunch with her. She is a lovely girl, who I would describe as my type of person. She's bubbly, funny, smart and the added bonus is her psychic abilities. I know a lot of people regard this kind of thing as hocus pocus, but I have always been drawn to people with spirituality and, although I don't live and die by readings, I still think it's interesting. I had a lovely brunch with Nicola, laughing at how awful the Dan situation was, as enough time had passed for us to see the funny side. She was definitely very hurt by him at the time, but she was also glad she had discovered he was a two-timing love rat.

We also talked about the dating landscape and what a jungle it is out there. We agreed it's very tricky to find the good ones who don't treat you like dirt. She also admitted it was hard to trust men again after the way Dan treated her. I said I would try and think of a good man to set her up with, as I do know some nice single men. They just tend to be single for a reason, such as they look for very specific types of girls – maybe sporty, dark-haired or younger than them. But once I had met Nicola I could see she was a beautiful person inside and out and would suit quite a few men I know.

She did a psychic reading for me, saying that my granddad on my dad's side had been standing by my side for the duration of our brunch. She described him perfectly. A tall, slim man, who was very intelligent and had a very gentle, happy demeanour. She said I was very close to my mum, but I was much more like my dad's side of the family. She said Grandad was telling her I needed to keep writing and everything was going to be fine. She said

I would see changes in May and that I would be moving possibly home and jobs. She said that the man front would improve and that I should just keep doing what I'm doing.

It was all very interesting and when she described my granddad, it sent a shiver down my spine. He died in 2012 and I honestly felt like he had been by my side. Who knows whether any of it will come true but I felt comforted by the words 'Keep writing'. Writing this particular story today has been yet another therapeutic means of detoxing my mind, this time of a man who tainted my dating journey. It's amazing how offloading this stuff is helping to clear my mind and clarify what's important. And what turned out to be Dan's loss became our gain.

ARTIST: Alexander O'Neal
TITLE: 'Fake'
REASON: Self-explanatory (also love this song).

Chapter 13

Be Careful What You Wish For

Today I have been thinking about some of the reasons why being single should be celebrated and not a torment. Sundays can be a bit hard when you're single at my age, as so many friends are quite rightly spending the day with their partners and/or young family. But it's also those friends who can be almost accusatory when they ask, 'How's the love life? *Still* looking for Mr Right?' It's just a big game to them; they are settled and happy and they know there are highs of going on dates. But they come with the lows of spending a lot of time on your own.

I remember getting the 'Sunday fear' when I was at school, as I knew I needed to get my homework done, iron my uniform and polish my shoes in time for Monday morning. But these days the fear is of having no one to hang out with and being reminded I am still single. And it got me thinking, What do I want? Well, Idris Elba is who I want, but sadly he's not available. So, second to Idris is a really hot man (with a sizeable manhood if poss!) who's kind, likes a laugh and wants to do stuff! Is that too much to ask?! However, sometimes I need to be careful what I wish for. It's now been two weeks since I last had sex. This might not sound like a long time, but it is for me. I honestly believe some people are more sexual than others, and sex is really important to me.

I was a late developer, not experiencing proper penetrative sex until I was nineteen. Considering there were girls at school who had already had abortions, I honestly felt like I was the last person on Earth to lose my virginity. However, I have made up for it since! The more I have, the more I want. But previously when there were dry spells I always had fuck-buddy James to rely on. The girls always consoled me with *Sex and the City*-style chit-chat about 'Mr Candle Cock'. There was never a very long period without intimacy until I put myself on my man detox. Instead of crying into my pillow, I've been thinking about the times when I got more than I bargained for.

James has always set the bar pretty high for me, as for years his size and ability to satisfy me have been incomparable. These were major reasons for him being a constant for seven or eight years. Then Henry arrived. I remember reeling off my man wish-list to a friend. The list was topped with 'kindness', followed by 'a sense of humour', 'tall' and a jokey 'massive cock' tagged on. Shortly after this conversation I swiped right on Henry.

Henry also worked in the media, had very handsome, natural-looking photos on his dating profile and was quick to message me when we matched. He was quick to tell me about a bizarre coincidence – we had a friend in common who he used to go out with. I felt a bit weird, so I quizzed him about it and he said their relationship was twenty years ago. Not ideal, but I thought it was still worth meeting him.

We had a drink in a swanky bar in Marylebone and he was dressed beautifully. He was far more dapper and gentlemanly in real life. He was tall. He was charm personified, with a great sense of humour, a big smile and gorgeous, kind eyes. We talked about past relationships and our careers and found we had a lot in common. After a few drinks, he quickly became very tactile and at the end of the night he walked me to the train station holding my hand. We got to the ticket barrier, where he dropped his bag to the ground in order to snog my face off. I was quite blown away, to be honest. Was Henry everything I had been wishing for?

Henry loved to phone me for chats, which I really like as it's hard getting to know someone over texts. He was a very sensitive chap and loved a cuddle. But he was a big guy and whenever he held me I felt secure in his arms and turned on by his hands. We went on a few dates, including a pub in the countryside, where we found a snuggly corner with leather sofas, so we could be that annoying smoochy couple you want to be sick over, canoodling in the corner.

He spent the whole night teasing his hand up my skirt, getting me more and more excited about what was to come. I drove him back to his tube station and we sat in the car, continuing to snog passionately and awkwardly over the front seats. I leant across the gear stick and felt his, which was rock-solid and ready to burst out of his trousers. I realised then I might have a big one to look forward to. I just told him we needed to wait until we'd been on a few more dates before it could be unleashed.

After a few more drinks and dinner dates I invited him to come to my house. I had my makeup done professionally, as I knew that night would be the one for 'third base'. I picked him up from the tube, the traffic was murderous and we had a much longer journey than we should've had. But it meant Henry had more time to continue with his tactile ways, nestling his hand between my legs at every opportunity. I loved feeling his giant hands on my inner thighs while I was still in control of the brake and accelerator. Tempers and temperatures were rising due to the traffic and heat of the summer but also the sexual tension between us.

We had barely stepped through my front door before we ripped each other's clothes off. In fact, I didn't even have a chance to unstrap my heels. What I hadn't quite prepared myself for was his rounders-bat-sized cock! I have never seen or felt anything like it. It was obscene and, well, breathtaking. I honestly think it bashed against my spine. When it came to changing positions, I was looking for an option to *not* insert it inside me. I started to go down on him and he told me his preference for me sucking his balls rather than his cock. For a split second I felt relieved, until I realised his giant balls were as obscene as his cock, and putting them inside my mouth was honestly like licking a rubbery, wrinkly elephant!

I thought Henry had it all, as he really made me laugh and I loved being in his company, but he really was an example of how you can be physically incompatible, sexually. We had a few more dates, but the initial sparkle between us dimmed after we'd had sex when really it should be the other way round. I mulled over the possibility that I had an odd-shaped vagina that was smaller than normal. I had never experienced this before.

I also caught up with our mutual friend, Sophie. They had, in fact, fallen out monumentally and it turned out their relationship wasn't quite so far in the distant past. They had rekindled it a few times over those twenty years, the last occasion being only recently and 'it didn't end well'. I also had the very honest conversation with Sophie about there being such a thing as 'too big' and she agreed. Very strange talking to one of your girlfriends about sleeping with the same man, especially on the subject of cock size. I'm sure most men would be grateful for this kind of accolade, but Henry's was verging on frightening! Needless to say, this love affair between Henry and me was fairly short-lived. We were incompatible on many levels and I have not been able to look at elephants in the same way since. There was no way I could have signed up for a lifetime of that!

ARTIST: Gorgon City featuring MNEK
TITLE: 'Ready for Your Love'
REASON: This just reminds me of Henry. Turns out I wasn't ready for his love!

Chapter 14

DB9 Man

Nearly a month into my man detox, I've been reflecting on some of the excitement I've had with men this year. This is not to torment myself about what I'm currently missing, but to work out whether I should just accept that it was what it was, or do I need to think that I messed up at the first hurdle?

I told a friend about the detox and she messaged me, 'You don't need to be off the market too long! Think of all the other girls snapping up those guys whilst you aren't available!' Well, that's one way of looking at it, but I hold on to the belief that what's meant for me won't pass me by. The thing with online dating is it allows for more chance meetings than in real life. I find that there aren't many day-to-day encounters now, particularly as I am in a routine of going to work, seeing colleagues and going to the same gym. Even in those situations where I might have once started to chatting to someone – on the train, say

– these days everyone is likely to be on their phones and/ or laptops. That's how I get pushed into a corner with the online dating game.

I have used a number of dating apps over the years – MySingleFriend, Tinder, Happn, Bumble and OkCupid. And I have a ridiculous addiction to seeing how many 'likes' I can get. Getting some stranger's endorsement of my face is flattering and gives me (false) confidence to keep trying to find Mr Right. As I have banished myself from all dating opportunities, I am not having endless chats with strangers and I am not putting myself through the heart-pounding first date 'Is it him or not?' moment at the bar. I admit that adrenaline-pumping moment can also be quite addictive, but that's the whole point of this detox – I'm a dating junkie in rehab.

What I think I started to lose sight of was whether the man was actually right for me and a potential boyfriend or husband (which is what I want) and not just a quick fix. One of these dates was with a man who I swiped right on by accident – easily done if your finger slips! On the basis of his pictures, I wouldn't normally have been keen. I am healthy but voluptuous and I hate feeling bigger than my man.

I could see from Faisal's photos he was very skinny and short. He was also a bit flashy and boasted about fast cars and clubbing in his pics and didn't have much chat. He didn't add a description to the photos, which I hate. I like to read a bit about a person before I start messaging them. However, when he asked me out for a drink very soon after matching, I thought, Why not? He told me where he lived in Kensington and I looked up his road on Google's street view and saw impressive, multi-million-pound homes with protruding bays and huge white columns flanking the front doors (gulp). I live in a modest flat and felt instantly out of my league, but he was insistent on coming to take me out near where I lived.

We arranged to meet at my local and as it was a nice evening I waited in the beer garden. Bang on time, a very flashy sports car pulled into the pub car park. I whispered under my breath, 'Fuck me.' He was very handsome, a lot taller than I expected, smelt of very expensive aftershave and made my heart skip a beat – perhaps a combination of first-date nerves and an instant attraction. We chatted about all sorts of nonsense over a huge gin and tonic: our backgrounds, education, jobs, family, etc. He was quick to tell me I was 'beautiful' and how much he loved my 'amazing eyes' (smooth!). I was slightly perturbed when he turned to the subject of sex very quickly. I tried to change the topic and suggested we go to a different pub, mainly because I wanted to drive in his amazing car. It was brand-new with that arousing new car smell and it turned out he had only had it a few weeks. At the next pub, he made a point of telling me about his property 'empire' and tight network of celeb mates (rolls eyes).

The more he talked, the more I realised I couldn't keep up with his financial and professional boasts, which meant I inadvertently gave him couldn't-care-less vibes and the impression that I wasn't interested in the slightest. So, of course he tried even harder. When it came to dropping me home, my heart sank. I didn't want him to see where I lived! He was a filthy-rich property tycoon with a hundred-thousand-pound Aston Martin DB9 (yes, he told me that) and I knew my neighbours' curtains would have been twitching if he revved that up outside my place. So, I directed him to a posh house adjacent to my flat.

We nattered in the car for a minute and then he leant over to kiss me. It was a very confident, sexy kiss, continuing for a good twenty minutes, before his hand started to move up my sundress. It was exhilarating. The combination of the stomach-churning, wheel-spinning car ride and his commanding kissing, hands everywhere, had left me quivering and soaking wet. But eventually I had to get out of the car, thinking to myself, If he's really interested, he can wait.

I sent him in the opposite direction to my flat and walked round the back of someone else's garage, waiting for him to disappear into the distance before I ran around to my actual home. Soon after the date he messaged, 'Thank you for a nice evening'. But he also 'unmatched' me on Bumble that night, which I knew was a sign he wasn't really interested and hadn't got what he wanted. But if I am completely honest with myself, I wasn't interested in him either. Mainly because in my heart of hearts I knew we were way too different. It was exciting and I'm glad we met, but 'DB9 Man' really was an example of how I need to stay true to myself. Essentially, I had been wowed by his impressive stature, but we had absolutely nothing in common and I was just flattered by him. To this day, I don't know if he knew I faked where I lived.

The episode made me giggle, but it wasn't exactly the grounds for a long and lasting relationship. It was exciting for one night, but when I think about what I'm missing out on during my man detox, this story reminds me that I don't need any more excitement like this. It's exhausting!

ARTIST: Go West
TITLE: 'King of Wishful Thinking'
REASON: I felt like I was in Richard Gere's car in *Pretty Woman*.

Chapter 15

Cruel to Be kind

Living in Bristol was a great experience for a number of reasons. I got to know a part of the UK where many born and bred residents were patriotic about their own city to the point of being oblivious to rest of the country, never mind the rest of the world. So many people have the attitude of 'Why do you need to be anywhere else?!'

It's a beautiful city, with a rich tapestry of architecture, cultures and cuisines, but so much so that a lot of people don't leave and have never left. My favourite date was with a guy called Sam, who I met on Tinder. He was a plumber from the town who seemed nice-looking and made it known in his profile he wanted to meet a woman to marry and have children with. I had just got back from living in LA and was keen to settle down too, so he seemed just the ticket. He told me that he owned his own house, teeth (ha, ha) and hair. The conversation started off like this:

SAM: Hi Verity! How are you doing? We matched! Are you having a good weekend?

ME: Yes, I'm good, thanks. I'm working a fair, but still getting to enjoy the sunshine.

SAM: I'm up early and off to a BBQ later. What do you do at the fair? Is it a dodgems-type fair?

ME: I'm working a fair bit, sorry missed the word 'bit'. Apologies!

SAM: Haha!

Following the miscommunicated message, Sam suggested we went for a drink and we made an arrangement to meet in a country pub between our homes. He sent me a few messages ahead of the date saying he was really looking forward to meeting me and also asked what I would be wearing. I thought that a bit weird and said (seeing as it was a regular Tuesday evening in the height of summer) that I would probably opt for a simple summer dress. In hindsight I think he just wanted to know what to look out for when I arrived. He texted me before I had even left home to ask me what I fancied to drink, and I said that I'd like my usual gin and tonic.

I pulled into the pub car park and immediately spotted a man sat in the pub garden with two G&Ts. My heart sank. He looked *nothing* like his profile pictures. They were all pretty vague, but none of them had been a true reflection of this – a large chap, with his gut hanging over his jeans and a mop of unwashed, sandy hair and thick sideburns. I looked in the rearview mirror at myself and had a stream of questions. Oh, fuck, not again? How could I have got it so wrong? Do I really have to go through with this? I thought, They say it's a numbers game... he might be the one... he seemed really nice in our messages... maybe I could fancy him...

As I sat there for what must have been thirty seconds but felt like thirty minutes, he spotted me in my car, looking in my mirror (hopefully he didn't see me swearing at myself) and started to wave. Yes, I did have to go through with this.

I walked over and he got up to greet me in his thick Bristol accent, 'Y'all right?' He was super-friendly and pulled out a chair out for me. He asked me about my day and it was all very pleasant. He wanted to hear about my background and I felt I was showing off by listing where I had lived and worked when he told me that he had never left Bristol. He was a bit wowed by the fact I had lived in London, never mind Hong Kong, Australia and the USA. Ultimately, I wanted where we had both lived and worked to be irrelevant, as we were both in the same place now, seemingly looking for the same thing.

About ten minutes into our chat, he leaned back on his chair with arms folded and paused for a minute, looking at me through slit-eyes. He piped up, 'Do you want to know what my mam and dad would say about you?'

Erm, I thought, No, not really. But instead I said, 'Go on...'

'My mam would say you've got child-bearin''ips, and my dad would say you've got a great pairuv tits.'

I could feel my face fill with a pink glow. WOW. That was a lot to hear so soon into the date. 'Err, thanks – I think.'

He made it known that he was keen to meet 'a good lady' to be his wife and the 'muvver of my kids'. Without any filter whatsoever, I think he was just describing what he saw. My child-bearing hips and boobs were an ideal fit.

Sam had previously sent me a random photo of a singer called Ben Howard. I had no idea who he was and looked him up ahead of the date so I was at least able to ask, 'Why did you send me a photo of Ben Howard? Do you want to go and see a gig or something?'

He was quick to say, 'Oh no – I'm growin' my 'air like Ben 'Oward, as I might lose all my hair soon through my chemo for my cancer, but it's OK, 'cos I've got sperm in da freeze.' Again, WOW. This was a *lot* of information for a first date. I honestly didn't know what to say, as I didn't know him well enough to know if he had a dark sense of humour or whether he was just laying all his cards on the table as time was running out for him to have a family. I tried to be sensitive with the information he had just given me but I was also in shock.

We had a laugh about how being a 'singleton' can be like having an extra head at times as we continued to chat for another twenty minutes or so, but I didn't pry too much into the cancer news, as I knew it would be a 'No' from me. Our pairing was not going to work. I had already known when I first laid eyes on him that I didn't fancy him. The unfiltered comments on my appearance and his monumental health news were not reasons for not getting together.

What we had in common was that we were both single and wanted to meet someone nice to do all the normal things in life, like buy a house and build a home for a family. I wanted the same things as him, but not with him. So, after less than an hour in total, I made my excuses and said I needed to get up early for work the next day – which was true. While I was driving the ten minutes home, I heard the beep of a text.

Sam: 'Hi Verity, thanks for a lovely evening, it was great to meet you. You are my cuppa tea you are, posh but naughty.'

Err... I wasn't sure how he gleaned that I was either posh or naughty from our chats, but there you have it. Funny what perceptions can be gained from so little time with a relative stranger who you initiated a meeting with by swiping right based on the look of their face. My point is: Sam and I had zero in common beyond the basics. We literally 'liked' each other's face, but apart from that, there was nothing organic about the process in which we met and our worlds were too far apart. Even though I must have been having a day when I wanted desperately to find a man who wanted marriage and children, there had to be more than that between us.

Sam hadn't been anywhere or done anything and had no intention of doing so. The result was that every time he asked me anything about myself and I opened my mouth he thought I was 'posh', because I had left Bristol and travelled the world, been to university and came from a family who did the same. I don't care what accent someone has, or where they come from, but when you have no common ground, it is hard to still fancy that face (which I didn't anyway). I often wonder what happened to Sam, but I did send a polite reply to say it had been nice to meet him, but there had been no spark for me. You aren't going to fancy everyone you meet in person. Sometimes you have to be cruel to be kind.

Man Detox

ARTIST: Shakira

TITLE: 'Hips Don't Lie'

REASON: Child-bearing hips don't lie!

Chapter 16

Relapse

I feel sick and my heart is pounding. I've relapsed. Why did I do it?

It's been a week since I received a message from Ben. But despite convincing myself I was doing the right thing by not replying, it has been tearing me apart. I didn't ever fall out with him. I just told him I couldn't be with him while he still lived with his ex. Nothing will have changed in such a short time.

I have come a long way in my man detox, but not replying to his message just felt rude and I felt like I wasn't being true to myself. One of the lessons I have been learning about me, myself and love through writing every day, is that there have been many occasions when I haven't been true to myself when it comes to messages.

I am emotional, I am loving and caring and I have very often been torn between what I think I should do versus what I really want to do. However, I should have also learned by now that my transparency and lack of mystery have not been helpful. Sending messages can be so destructive at times, as I probably say too much and then wait by the phone for a response that is often not the one I want. The number of times I have pressed 'send' leaving my stomach doing somersaults... But I wonder if caving into hitting that send button does me any favours, and could be a reason why it hasn't worked out with certain men.

One of those men was Simon. He stood out on his Bumble profile for wearing a suit in every photo. In fact, my opening gambit (as the girl has to open the conversation on Bumble) was, 'You seem to be a fan of a blue blazer?' He immediately replied with a suitably confident, 'You seem to be a fan of me.' We started chatting over messages and he was quick to say he preferred to talk over the phone rather than text. He sounded like a proper grown-up. He had a very successful recruitment firm, which he had started and grown over twenty-five years. He was going through a divorce and had three children.

On our first date he met me at my local, arriving in his brand-new Mercedes and chivalrously getting out of the car to open the door for me. He was bald, with kind blue eyes and was very physically fit due to his passion for boxing. He suggested we went to a nicer, more upmarket bar. We got on brilliantly and despite it being a week day, we went to three different bars, drinking several double gin and tonics along the way. By the time we got to the third bar, he stopped outside and kissed me. He had amazing soft lips and gave me a very tender kiss, gently pressing the back of his fingers under my chin. That third bar was lavish, with low velvet sofas and soft lighting and we snuggled up in the corner and carried on kissing.

Simon told me he had only been on one other date since he had split up with his wife a year before. This woman had alarmed him on the first date by going to the loo to send him a pussy pic. He hadn't asked for it and she hadn't prepared him. He said it was too much and made his excuses. It gave me the impression he wasn't really keen on the way some women operate in the world of digital dating. He said he was old-fashioned after such a long relationship.

The last bar was five minutes away from Simon's house. He had told me that he lived in a bachelor pad that he shared with a mate who had also left his wife. They were a poor man's, forty-something *Men Behaving Badly*, except they carried the financial burden and responsibility of having ex-wives and children. I was drunk, but not that drunk, so agreed to go back for 'coffee'. Of course, there was no coffee. We went in the lounge, where he had a sparse arrangement of expensive-looking furniture (no pictures on the walls; the place needed a woman's touch), including a vast corner sofa onto which he nudged me as we snogged each other's faces off like teenagers.

Within twenty minutes of being at his house, I popped to the loo and came back to the lounge to find he was completely naked in front of me with a rock solid hard-on. Confident or what! I was still fully clothed and told him I didn't want to sleep with him on a first date. We rolled around on the sofa with him naked, pressing his hard cock against my sodden gusset. He was very sexy and there was definitely a difference between men who have been 'making love' in a marriage for twenty-five years and younger, inexperienced 'fuckers'.

He grabbed my hand and took me into his bedroom. Despite my reticence, he had done a very good job of luring me into his lair. We had the most amazing sex, orgasm after orgasm, all night long. I tried to leave, but he got hard again and again and encouraged some questionable acrobatics. I swear that Simon must have taken Viagra. He was so horny the whole time I was with him. We would meet for coffee, dinner, cinema, walks and the passion between us was electric, every time. Until one day, he went a bit quiet. He said he'd been ill and so I offered to go to his house with get-well remedies and soup, etc. He declined and gut instinct told me that was it, it was over. I was sure he was ill, but I noticed that he had also cooled off in his messages.

I was absolutely distraught following such an intense six-week period. It had been a whirlwind, being spoiled by an adoring man. He told me at any given opportunity how beautiful I was and always wanted to hold me, kiss me and turn me on. He had shown signs he was interested in something long-term, asking about my living arrangements and coming up with holiday plans.

When I don't understand a guy's change of heart, I often reach out to my brother, as he is great at giving me a male perspective and also knows me inside out. I told him the situation with Simon and asked him what I should do. My brother replied, 'You have to take control of your happiness now. It's not up to Simon to secure your happiness. It's you. Your behaviour. Your positivity. He's lucky to have you! Not the other way around. Be the boss!' I liked the idea of this, but it was very hard to carry out in practice.

I desperately wanted to know if Simon was OK. I could see he was online on WhatsApp, which suggested he wasn't *that* ill. I sent him many messages, trying to keep us communicating. Some he replied to, many he didn't. Eventually he wrote, 'V, I'm happy to meet up etc., but I want to be honest as well. I really can't commit to a relationship at the moment. With my divorce being finalised in the next few weeks and finding a home for my kids plus trying to work etc. I'm getting very swamped with stuff! Probably what's made me ill etc., LOL. Hope that's OK with you, but rather tell you upfront that I'm juggling lots of balls. I'll leave it with you. Take care, Simon.'

Ouch! Just writing about this has brought back all of those gut-wrenching feelings. How had I got so emotionally attached to someone who friend-zoned me and just saw me as a bit of fun? I wanted to reply with this: 'OK, thanks for letting me know. I thought we had a great connection, which doesn't come along that often. But I also would like to meet someone who has time for me, in addition to the rest of their life. I don't think that's too much to ask. Take care, Vx.' Instead, I sent, 'OK, cool, thanks for your honesty.' This message took me three hours to construct. It couldn't have been further from what I was feeling. I was anything but cool. I was distraught, curled up in the foetal position on my bedroom floor, looking like Alice Cooper, tears and mascara streaming down my face. I consoled myself with the fact he was just a bit of fun and he wasn't right for me. Until, a few days later, I had a couple of glasses of Prosecco and did the dreaded drink-and-dial, sending, 'I miss your massive cock.'

Oh dear.

He replied saying, 'Love the directness, V.'

I was such an absolute idiot. Not only had I bombarded him with messages while he was ill, but I had metaphorically thrown myself at him in the form of a drunken text message. Disastrous.

The point of this story, and many more like it, is that I was far more brazen and direct in messages than I would ever be in person. As with Chris (Chapter 8, *Hot Dogs and Kittens*) I didn't really ever let Simon know how much he hurt me. The outcome probably wouldn't have been any different, as he made it clear he didn't want a relationship. But writing this down makes me realise I should have implemented my man-detox text ban a long time ago. In fact, I think there should be a man-detox phone number for people like me to send messages to instead of the actual person.

Today's relapse was slightly different. Controversially, I sent a message to Ben, a week after he sent me his. I am coming to terms with the fact that I am not going to be with him, so I didn't want to be rude by not replying to him. I simply said: 'I miss you like crazy. I hope you're well xx'

I can hear you screaming at my book, saying, '*Noo!*'

He replied immediately, 'Ditto, how are you? Are you well? xx'

I realise I have broken my own detox rules here, but the point is that I wasn't being true to myself by not replying to him. He doesn't know I'm doing this man

Relapse

detox. I am not going to be with him, so what's the point in playing games? We have mutual friends and are very likely to see each other again. And ultimately, I feel better. I have cleared my conscience. It's not like I slept with him and nor will I, as this was only a relapse and tomorrow is a new day.

ARTIST: Daniel Caesar featuring H.E.R.
TITLE: 'Best Part'
REASON: Our song. Both Ben and I adore it and it will always be hard to hear it.

Chapter 17

Pretty Woman

I heard from Bloody Maria today. She is definitely one of those friends who lives vicariously through the single me. I'll be busy waffling on about my latest beau and she'll chip in with, 'Do you remember the man who...?' They are all just funny anecdotes to her.

Just to remind you, Bloody Maria is the one who went on *one* online date, married him and is now living happily ever after. The digital-dater's dream! Some of us have swiped hundreds of times and are effectively sifting through the silt of the dating world in an honest/desperate bid to snare a good man.

As I hurtle into the second month of this man detox, I can't help but feel a little bitter about some of the low-life vermin I have encountered online. I think, like most people, there is a huge element of hope involved in putting your face on a digital platform to meet 'the one'. I will always ask the man pretty early on what they are looking for, as many will say something 'hilarious' online, like: 'I've known Dave for forty years, he is kind, funny and has the whole package. Great cook, loves to travel and is looking for that good connection with the right person. If you are looking for great chat, great food and a great guy, then look no further and swipe right. Dave's Mum.' This is textbook online dating profile puff. I'm sure Dave is great – according to his mum. But is he going to take me on a few dates, promise me the world, get my hopes up and then suddenly stop communicating and fuck off to meet the next online potential match? I doubt many men would reveal to their mum they have behaved like that.

Having a bloke endorsed by his mum on a dating profile is almost as bad as the guys who describe themselves as if they're a secondhand car: 'Couple of previous owners, gear stick intact, needs regular servicing.' Give me strength! I have had my fair share of horrors, as Bloody Maria loves to remind me.

Take Cory, for example. He was, according to his photos, nothing short of drop-dead gorgeous. The muscles bulged from his tight T-shirts, and were also shown off in the flawless topless shots. However, in all of them you couldn't quite make out his face. When I swiped right, I couldn't believe we had matched. Why would he be interested in geeky old me?! He said he was Australian and thirty-four, four years younger than me at the time, but as my friend Rachel says, 'It's good to catch them young!' She thinks they are less corrupted when they are younger, like some sort of pristine disk drive! But in my experience, it's the other way round. The younger they are, the more sordid they can be, as they have only ever known dating in the digital world and everything and anything is fair game. In our instant messaging chat, Cory was quick to tell me what he thought of me...

ME: Hi Cory! Great pics!

CORY: Hi Variety, lovely to Tinderise with u. U R very beautiful lady. Nices to hear from you. [I chose to ignore him misspelling my name. I have had a lifetime of being called 'Variety', mainly due to autocorrect. Verity is an unusual name and I am often called Clarity, Charity, Chastity, Dorothy, etc.]

ME: Have you had a good weekend?

CORY: You have amazing eyes and smile that could warm a room. Have you found your lobster yet? You look so sexy.

ME: I've found a few crustaceans and a few nobsters... but no lobsters! Thanks. What do you do for a living?

CORY: Work in the City for a hedge fund.

ME: Ah cool, I have a few mates who do that.

CORY: Nice. Whereabout London R U from?

ME: West.

CORY: ok, I'm Chelsea.

ME: How have you found Tinder?

CORY: Tinder is amazing, it has many lovely girls here. It's obvious why amazing – not amazing for you? Why are you single? You're absolutely stunning.

ME: Thanks. Well, pictures tell a thousand words, but I always think it's better to meet.

CORY: Me too. But I want to ask you something.

ME: OK.

CORY: Would you meet me in a hotel?

ME: Depends where?

CORY: ok so here goes... i have had a fantasy for a while now where i find it very exciting and such a big turn on at the thought of me offering a very beautiful and tremendously sexy girl like you a once in a lifetime offer. The offer be that i offer you a sum of money for us to have some fun at a nice hotel. I am not into anything weird odd or kinky and i have a great job and career and would treat you with the most amount of respect throughout. Let me know your thoughts and potentially how much you would want. I was think between £2000-£3000 for the night but open for you to suggest...

ME: Wow, I didn't expect that.

CORY: Have a think about it.

I thought about it for about a millisecond and thought, Absolutely not, you disgusting human being. I did not spend four years at university to become an expert in my field to become fucking *Pretty Woman*! He could have been anyone! He could have been a gang who wanted to rape me. Anything could have happened. So many thoughts passed through my head. I decided to post about this noxious offer on Facebook and the responses were incredible:

SJB: 'Oh, Cory! And your picture looks quite promising! Stick with it, Verity – your prince is out there amongst those crazy nutjobs!'

NS: 'I'd drive you for a cut of the money.'

CA: 'Ew! How miserable.'

AL: 'He sounds like a charmer! WTF is wrong with people!'

RJ: 'I'm in! And I want the full three grand! No bargaining!'

VF: 'Three grand plus a nice, black cocktail dress! And some fancy cutlery lessons! Wait a sec – I've seen that somewhere before.'

HG: 'Does he have an age limit? Assuming the hotel is the Dorchester?'

EL: 'Does he mind what gender? LOL.'

AV: 'Oh my God! What the hell?!'

CA: 'Madonna Mia. I think he's copied and pasted that a good few times! Block immediately!'

NP: 'Wow. But don't worry – he's got a great job. That makes it absolutely OK.'

SJ: 'What the actual fuck?! Not a weirdo, my arse!'

PP: 'I'll do it.'

NA: 'Jeez! I think you should arrange to meet him and send a very manly drag queen in your place, saying your pic wasn't an accurate one, to teach him a lesson!'

MC: 'I'm in for fifty per cent.'

JD: 'Wow. The most I've ever been offered was a hundred pounds.'

HE: 'Tell him there's a whole other site for stuff like that! Literally no words any more.'

CW: 'Good grief, some men are just gross, aren't they?! So sorry you have to put up with this shit. Did you report him?'

AW: 'OMG!'

MA: 'Wow. Mx'

JG: 'Wow, what an idiot x'

JB: 'Tell me that's not for real?!'

BH: 'Oh, Verity!!! Another great one x'

KM: 'OMG! I experienced some weird stuff too, amazing the freaks out there! Some nice ones too though. x'

CH: 'That's awful, V. x'

JW: 'Cory sounds like a stand-up guy and I think you should broaden your horizons.'

TS: 'Oh, I've had this too! That's why I've given up on dating apps – they're all (OK, mostly) weirdos!'

SH: 'My friend has exactly the same message.'

DA: 'OMG, what in the name...?!'

PW: I would do this for sixty to seventy pounds. Could you pass on his details?'

SG: 'What price did you agree on?'

JO: 'Bloody hell, V!'

JK: 'Oh my dear God! He's the one! xxx'

AP: 'Sounds like that film! With Demi Moore! X'

JA: 'He thinks he's Robert Redford. He needs to watch the film again. I'm pretty sure the going rate was a hundred thousand dollars!'

NF: 'Shit, man, he's probably a people trafficker?! Using such tactics to weed out the vulnerable and (financially) desperate. Scumbag. I'd report it, you don't know the motives of some people and this is massively suspect.'

TF: 'Seriously?! Oh my God. Words fail me.'

JT: 'Two to three thousand pounds? Does he know you are gold x'

RH: 'Would he accept a married mum of two instead?? Desperate times an' all.'

CT: 'I was thinking the same.'

PB: 'His name's Cory FFS. Only consider if you'd shag a Trevor or any variation of Shane, Dwayne or Wayne. And then only if he's wearing a suit.'

AM: 'Nob!! X'

IC: 'You had me at OK ... I'd throw in a cup of tea as well.'

AC: 'OMG is all I can say. How many syllables did you reply back to him with? That's if you could be bothered!'

KB: 'Money up front!'

JW: 'Do it!'

SE: 'Dear God.'

MC: 'Awful. You wanted at least five thousand pounds, right? x'

NW: 'I'm so glad you shared, Verity. The comments on here are hilarious!'

SC: 'Blimey.'

JP: 'Hey, but he'd treat you with the utmost respect while treating you like a prostitute simultaneously. Am sure he should be fucking locked up!! So wrong!! Xx'

CW: 'Hang on, this is awful! There was no mention of hotel options, transport requirements. Was breakfast included? Should you take your gym kit? Crazy! Plus he wrote this at 9.58 a.m. – Casanova.'

PT: 'Hardly Robert Redford, but two to three thousand pounds is not to be sniffed at. With two thousand pounds you could buy 743 McDonald's cheeseburgers, 2,500 Lion bars; 625 pints of beer (487 if you're in London); 952 quiche lorraines from Sainsbury's.'

JD: 'WTFingF?? But I could do with two thousand pounds about now so...'

AS: 'I'd let him do anything he likes to me for that cash.'

WW: 'What a catch!'

AR: 'There are some really horrible and creepy people out there. Why would anyone think that was normal behaviour?'

There were hundreds more messages, all of a similar ilk. It was not what I imagined, almost a human nature experiment through the power of social media. Bear in mind that I was in complete shock. I wanted some sympathy, which I got, but I also got a lot of people seeing the funny side, which was also fine. However, it made me realise there are probably people who have accepted Cory's offer and it would be interesting to know what happened. Could I have done anything differently? Were the 'catfish' warning signs there from the outset? I had immediately spotted the broken English and spelling mistakes but gave him the benefit of the doubt. I was way too scared to reply, wondering if he was somehow infiltrating my dating profile and stealing my identity or something. As soon as I'd taken a screenshot of the 'offer', I deleted the conversation and removed him from my matches. Cory was just another nail in the coffin of online dating experiences that made me question if apps are a sad indictment of the digital age as opposed to an example of liberation for the twenty-first century.

I'm glad it gave so many of my friends some amusement, but I was still quite shocked it happened. At least it gave

Pretty Woman

Bloody Maria another story to pass to her bore-off housewife mates, but it was definitely a toxic experience and I am glad to dispose of it in my man detox. No matter how long it takes for me to find a good man, I would never stoop that low. This isn't a Hollywood movie – this is my real life!

ARTIST: Jessie J
TITLE: 'Price Tag'
REASON: It is definitely not about money!
You can't afford me.

Chapter 18

What's Porn Got to Do with It?

I don't remember Tina Turner ever singing 'What's porn got to do it with it?' but it should be a modern version of her song.

Whether I like it or not, porn is a massive part of twenty-first-century society. I personally have never indulged, as I just don't get turned on by watching other people have sex. Particularly as so much of the time, it's just acting. Also, I get too upset thinking about the slave labour that goes on in the sex industry. I very much doubt that a hundred per cent of the people starring in pornography are enjoying their dream vocation in life.

I have a few friends (men and women) who tell me it is a daily activity: 'wanking to porn'. But I've also had experiences with guys who have not so much lost their inhibitions having watched a lot of it but have become terribly insecure because of what they've seen on screen. The expectation to reenact porn scenes is more common.

This for me is a toxic element of dating. I wish I could believe it was just liberating, sexual exploration, but some things are just murky.

Last year, I was having a break from men, but as usual it lasted about five days. (It's 1 December as I write this and I can't believe I've made it to the second month of my man detox!) My break followed a series of ghostings and I'd promised myself I wasn't going to let that happen again. When I dated again, I went for a geek. Tom was five years younger than me, but he seemed mature. He was a surveyor, working in the City, and his Bumble profile included pics of him shooting and wearing a Barbour with his family, and all his pics were safe. By this, I mean, there were none of him topless or selfies in the mirror that would suggest he had no friends to take pictures or images of him holding dumbbells the size of cars or suggestive pants/cock-shots.

We arranged to meet for a drink in town, in a pretty average old man's pub near his office in Westminster after work one night. He was much younger in the flesh, despite a receding hairline, and was very smartly dressed in a suit with shiny shoes. He told me he preferred older women with something to grab hold of. We chatted easily and laughed a lot and he was very easy company and quite handsy quite quickly. I didn't think I was that enamoured by him and then he kissed me, in the bar. I was quite taken aback, as he had appeared to be quite straitlaced up to this point.

We then got on to the subject of Pussy Galore, an 'exclusive' sex club which I have never been to. It's not widely known but I had heard about it through a friend. It was only certain people who go there, which we discussed. He had been taken there by an older woman on a date, which left me slightly unnerved (red flag). Why would he want to intimate he had been gang-banging in an underground sex club? After much chat about life, love and sex, we had established a good connection by the end of the night. We parted company by snogging each other's faces off at the top of the steps of the tube, him slipping his hand down my jeans onto my bare, cold bottom. It felt exciting, maybe the start of something special, and I got on the tube home with a spring in my stride!

We continued to chit-chat over messages and he said he was keen to cook for me in his new flat he'd bought thanks to a handout from his dad. He said he'd perfected a roast dinner (all right, Jamie Oliver!) and insisted I should go to his for a Sunday afternoon roast. But when I rang the buzzer at the communal front door he didn't answer. It was freezing, so I WhatsApped him to say I had arrived. Still nothing. While I was standing there, a neighbour unlocked the door to go into the block of flats and held the door open for me.

I found Tom's flat on the third floor and knocked on the door. Still no answer. I was on time and I was sure it was the right flat. I pressed my ear up against the door and could hear the shower. I waited until I could hear the water turn off. I knocked gingerly and he came to the door soaking wet, with a towel wrapped around his bottom half.

I love seeing a man who's straight out of the shower – they look so sexy with wet skin, especially if the drops of water are falling into the grooves of a hot six-pack. Tom didn't have the greatest body and had bigger love handles than I expected but I still fancied him. He took me into the lounge and offered me a drink. I said not to worry until he'd got dressed. I was sat on his very low sofa and he bowed over me and whispered, 'I might not bother getting dressed.'

He started kissing me pretty much immediately and let his towel drop to the floor. He was hard and bald – completely bald – downstairs. I'm used to manscaping, but this was a new level. There wasn't a single hair in sight. I said to him, 'You're freshly trimmed' and he said, 'Oh, yes, I love a freshly shaved scrotum.' For a brief moment, I thought, Your own scrotum? How many scrotums have you seen (red flag)?

He was quick to dry off by rubbing against me while kissing me on the sofa and he started to undress me. He held my hand and took me, dressed just in my underwear, into his bedroom. It was a brand-new, spacious apartment with crisp white sheets on a king-size bed. He pushed me backwards onto the bed. He said this was the spare bedroom as he 'needed to change the sheets' on his own bed. More alarm bells went off, as I thought, I wonder who else has been in his bed? He pushed my legs apart and knelt down to lick me out. He spat on my pussy even though I was already wet and, when you don't know a guy, this can be pretty violating and is far from sexy. In my experience, it can also cause an irritation if there's a pH imbalance between the spittle and the vagina. He was also pretty vigorous and he asked me if I was turned on. I had made noises to suggest I was, but I was a long way from a fully-fledged orgasm.

I returned the favour and found it pretty rough around my lips where he had pubic stubble. Not only had his shaving made his penis and balls look like uncooked meat but I could feel my lips burning as if I'd been licking a plucked chicken. He reached down under the bed and pulled out handcuffs and the most enormous black dildo I have ever seen. It was like a police baton that you might see armed police use in footage of '80s protests. He said, 'Would you like me to tie you up and tantalise you with my toy?' I declined and said I'd prefer to have a go on his own, natural weapon.

His penis was average and not that hard, but maybe I've been spoiled with other men. We tried many positions including sixty-nine, standing, missionary, wheelbarrow, spooning and doggy, but even when I was on top, which usually guarantees an orgasm, it was unsatisfying. We were just completely out of sync with each other and his bottom slaps were too hard and not rhythmic. They were off-putting and distracting rather than sexy.

After he had finished, spunking all over my chest, we were lying on the bed side-by-side, with little after-care from him. No cuddles, no interest in touching or kissing. It was like he'd just finished a (poor) acting performance. He then asked me if he was big enough and what I was used to. He told me he liked to use his toy on himself. I didn't ask too much, but essentially I got the impression he was very keen on using the dildo, as he'd seen it in pornos. This was when it dawned on me what was happening here. It turned out he was absolutely addicted to porn and had been heavily influenced by watching. The hair-free anatomy, the pussy-spitting, the dildo up his arse, the heavy-handed spanking and the acrobatic positions were what he was watching on screen every day – and this is what he expected in the bedroom from a woman.

We got dressed and although it wasn't awkward between us, it wasn't romantic either. He hadn't even gone into the kitchen yet to put his much-hyped chicken in the oven and I told him I needed to get going before it would be ready. He tried to convince me to stay and said his 'demon roast' was worth the wait. But when I made my excuses, he started to probe me about his performance in the bedroom. He kept asking if he was big enough, if was he satisfying, if he was hard enough compared to other guys I'd been with. I just flipped it back at him, asking why he was worried and where these deep insecurities were coming from. Again, he made reference to seeing much larger cocks on porn. I assured him I hadn't been thinking about that and said if I spent my whole time comparing myself to skinny, polished porn stars, I wouldn't ever have the confidence to have sex.

The whole experience with Tom was a strange one, but being with him wasn't the only occasion I've encountered a guy who has become so warped by what he has seen on porn. To watch or not is a personal choice, but I am totally convinced that porn, to this extreme, is not helping people like me forge the foundations for a happy, healthy, natural relationship. Yes, I'm happy to be open-minded and be adventurous in the bedroom, but the whole experience had been soulless and left me feeling empty. I didn't hear from Tom again, but then I didn't contact him either. This is definitely one of those online dating experiences that convince me I am absolutely fine to take a break from men and, going forward, take notice of the red flags!

ARTIST: Tina Turner
TITLE: 'What's Love Got to Do with It'
REASON: As above!

Chapter 19

Maneater

It's now 2 December and I have come so far with my man detox that I have decided to carry on.

Some of my friends are saying I should call this month DEmenBER, but I'm not trying to win any awards for changing the months of the year to suit my detox. It's more that I have so many more stories I want to offload, plus it's making me feel a million times better about life, love and the universe! However, I am a self-confessed horny lady and when you are depriving yourself of the one thing you love most, it's very hard not to daydream. I am stopping myself from contacting any men who are potential dates or sex. However, I didn't ever promise not to 'self-love'!

I first discovered the euphoria of masturbation quite late on, at university at the grand old age of nineteen. Ancient, considering boys I grew up with had been caught wanking aged eleven. Yes, admittedly, it's pretty antisocial to be caught red-handed at school. This was coupled with the fact that my brother once got grounded after my mum caught him knocking one out, and it made me steer clear of touching myself intimately. It wasn't until I was older that I realised that making yourself orgasm is not dirty when it's done in the privacy of your own home, it's natural. I think I was late to the party with self-exploration!

It's another memory that comes hand-in-hand with a song, one I happened to hear on a film soundtrack at the time. It was *Runaway Bride* with Julia Roberts. It was a pretty average film, but I really liked the soundtrack and it was playing on my '90s CD hi-fi stack in my university halls on the night that, for some reason, I first decided to touch myself. I was in typical student mode: an incense stick was burning, it was dark, and the song from the soundtrack was 'Maneater' by Hall & Oates. I'm sure you're thinking that this is pretty apt for me, but it's not so much to do with the lyrics as the harmonies and beats of the song.

It starts with that iconic bass guitar and then synthesiser, acoustic guitar and saxophone are layered over the top. It literally struck a chord with me! I used two fingers, rubbing them against my clitoris, and I gave myself the most powerful orgasm, the fuzzy feeling vibrating through my body from head to toe. Weird that there was a song playing when I first made myself orgasm but there was and that was it. The musical composition just makes me tingle all over every time I hear it.

I remember sitting down at the kitchen table when I was around fourteen and asking my mum what an orgasm was like. This makes me shudder, just thinking how bold I was to do this. My mum was actually very good at being matter-of-fact about it. She just said it was an amazing feeling you can get from deep inside, a little like the feeling when you really need the loo, but nicer than that. This still springs to mind as it's a fairly accurate description, but I would add that it's like popping candy going off at the same time! There is also a different intensity to the orgasm depending on whether it's vaginal or clitoral. I've already mentioned I am not interested in porn as stimulation but I do always have someone on my mind. Sometimes multiple men! But there is one man who always springs to mind, often at the crucial moment of climax as he gave me one of the best penetrative orgasms I've ever had.

Bobby was my boss some time ago. When I first met him he appeared to be quite shy, reserved and insular. He was a big man with a penchant for beer and curry, and extremely talented at his job. There's something very arousing about a man who commands a newsroom/radio station. Bobby was very polite towards me but I always took the stance that if I didn't hear anything about my work from him, he must be happy. I just regarded him as a figure of authority at work and nothing else.

After getting into the groove of my job I was able to use my creativity in my reporting style. I remember I went out and did a report about 'flirting at the traffic lights' as a survey had come out 'revealing' the number of people who had met while waiting. It was a local radio story and it would be localised for our demographic. The original headline read something like, PEOPLE IN DERBYSHIRE AND NORTH LEICESTERSHIRE ARE FINDING LOVE AT THE TRAFFIC LIGHTS. In reality, the people in this region were no more likely to meet people at the traffic than people in London or Timbuktu, but it made listeners of the breakfast show in their cars in the morning think it was a story about them, which is the art of local radio.

I went out with a Dictaphone and recorded myself describing what was happening when I got to the traffic lights. It was a typical local radio package with cheesy 'Je T'Aime' music at the start interrupted by the sound of car horns and me setting the scene: 'I'm at a set of busy traffic lights in the city centre, testing out these bold claims being made by this survey, that twelve per cent of couples meet at the traffic lights.' The piece included me trying to get men's attention by pulling up next to men in white vans, single men in their cars and lorries. It took a few attempts but eventually I got a few wolf whistles, car horns and eventually a phone number. The whole thing was very tongue-in-cheek, but it was fun and encouraged listeners to get in touch with their own stories of how they had met their partners. None at the traffic lights, I might add!

The next day, Bobby came over to me to congratulate me, but also to give me a ribbing about 'award-winning journalism on such essential news'. For the first time he was so friendly, he was verging on flirty. It seemed my report had ignited something inside. Further banter in the newsroom involved him bringing up the subject of my 'pulling expertise' at any given opportunity. In his eyes I had become the 'romance reporter' – even though I only ever wanted to be known for unearthing compelling, original news stories!

When I left the radio station, I stayed in touch with Bobby, mainly because I needed to keep his details for a reference. One day he emailed that he was going to be in London for meetings and did I fancy meeting for a catch-up? This was totally unexpected but also flattering. He gave me the details of a posh hotel near Marble Arch and I made my way there for the 9 p.m. invite. Bobby had been at a boozy industry lunch and when I met him in the hotel lobby, his tie was skew-whiff and his hair was a bit all over the place, but he still looked nice in his suit. We sat in the beautiful art-deco bar, decadently drinking a bottle of champagne that he kindly bought.

We chatted freely about all the fun times at the radio station, the people we had worked with and he also told me how much everyone missed me. It was at this point his hand edged onto my knee. I was strangely enamoured by this, as he hadn't ever been tactile with me before. It would have been inappropriate at work. He was my boss! But he wasn't any more, so it seemed legitimate. I knew that he had a young son, but I had heard he was no longer with the child's mother. He asked me if I had been using my Romance Reporter expertise for my own love life and I just coyly brushed away the question, saying I was 'still Bridget Jones'. He asked if I also wore Bridget knickers – large ones. I was embarrassed but at the same time enjoying him asking me such out-of-bounds questions.

I felt suitably lubricated by the champagne and boldly asked, 'What made you invite me here tonight?'

He looked a bit cowardly before saying, 'I wanted to get to know you better.' I could see he was testing the water and I was flattered. This chat opened up a more candid conversation about how he always 'admired my work' but it had not been appropriate to contact me while I was working for him. But now I had left he had free reign to 'get to know me'.

After another bottle of champagne it was past midnight and he asked me if I wanted to stay at the hotel. He said there were two double beds in the room, so 'it wasn't a problem'. When we got to the room I saw there *were* two doubles, but they were queens pushed together. I had not planned on this and told him I didn't have a toothbrush or any vitals with me. He called the concierge and got them to bring up a vanity case. He did everything he could to make me feel comfortable, including putting on the TV with a 'retro' music channel. We sat on the bed and drank some miniatures from the mini-bar and laughed at the terrible music videos. And then, you guessed it, Hall & Oates' 'Maneater' came on.

It was at this moment Bobby tried his luck and reached around to kiss me. It was such a lovely evening that had resulted in this inevitable kiss. We kissed for the entirety of the song and I kept to myself why this song meant so much to me. But of course, it made me even more turned on in the heat of the moment, with a man who had been out-of-bounds and also not on my radar for years. He was a very passionate kisser and this led to the passionate kissing of the rest of my body. He was so attentive and he made sure every inch of my body was licked, stroked or kissed. By the time he reached for a condom and got ready to insert himself in me I was a gooey mess.

The sex was as amazing as the foreplay: he was so in tune with my body and we just fitted together harmoniously. This paved the way for orgasm after orgasm for me. I think the combination of our history as colleagues and the fact he had been my manager meant we were both ripping down the barricades in one fell swoop. Neither of us had planned this, so it was such a nice surprise when the chemistry, and in turn the sex, was unexpectedly electrifying. He said over and over again, 'That was amazing.' We had crossed previously forbidden, unchartered waters and given each other mutual, earth-shattering moments. To this day he was some of the best sex I've ever had and I think he sparked something new inside me, quite literally! I feel so sorry for women who can't orgasm from penetrative sex, as it's so amazing!

Although it would have been nice to repeat this whole affair, I think we both knew when we said goodbye the next day that it would never happen again. It was the thrill of the chase and spontaneity of the whole night that made it so exciting. When I think about how many of my friends have done that completely normal thing of meeting a guy through their jobs, I can't help but question my choices of work romances. But in a way, Bobby served his purpose as I still to this day think about him at the crucial moment of climax. Maybe I shouldn't have been so keen to see what else was out there and perhaps I should have pursued something more meaningful with him. Instead, I seemed to have lived up to my song after all.

ARTIST: Hall & Oates
TITLE: 'Maneater'
REASON: My song!

Chapter 20

On Demand

There have been several ongoing questions during my man detox, such as 'What can I learn from the experiences I have had with men?' and 'Could I have behaved differently and be married with children by now?' But a big one is: 'Am I a hussy or am I a victim of the current dating climate?'

Have I contributed to the soulless world of disposable dating? I have a wide group of friends – happily married ones, long-term relationship ones, perfectly happy single (not had sex for years) ones and then the multi-dating ones. Until 1 November, before NOmenBER kicked in, I was one of those, bumbling along, dating multiple guys. But are we as women responsible for the way men treat women online?

Only yesterday a friend of mine said she 'hated' the world of dating and yet had got really drunk on Saturday night and 'ended up fucking a guy from Tinder'. This is so common in the kingdom of singledom: it's pretty much the norm. But are women normalising what is essentially the Amazon Prime of dating? Men don't even need to wine and dine us. Just 'match and fuck' – it all happens in a matter of hours. I can't help but think, What the hell would my nan think? She courted my granddad for a year, meeting once a week at the pictures, before she let him 'bother her', as she called it!

I don't want to go back to the 1940s for many reasons, but on the other hand I think I would like to try being treated like a lady and made to feel special by a man courting me. I often put myself in a dreamscape in which I've got victory rolls in my hair and I'm wearing a beautiful fur coat, standing on a platform next to a steam train. An exquisitely turned-out man in a bowler hat and suit arrives, scoops me up, and says 'You're the woman of my dreams' and we live happily ever after. I bet she didn't go online, swipe right and shag a stranger.

I blame our on-demand culture. If you want something, you order it. Gone are the days of going to the Blockbuster shop to rent a video – you just watch on demand. Order any cuisine you desire and it can be on your lap within the hour. In fact, thanks to the likes of Amazon Prime, you can have pretty much anything delivered to your door within hours. You don't have to wait for it or earn it. And this is pretty much the same in the dating world.

Only once have I done on-demand dating. I would never intentionally plan to fuck a man and never see them again. However, it did happen. I matched with a guy called Adam on Bumble. He looked absolutely gorgeous. A chiselled model with sandy hair, blue eyes, long eyelashes and an amazing body. Basically, he was out of my league. Pretty much immediately he asked for my number, so he could WhatsApp and arrange to meet. He wasted no time in sending a very impressive cock pic and simply asked: 'You want it? You like the size? What are you up to tonight?' I said I was busy and he asked me if I lived alone. I was quick to tell him I had a flat mate. I thought to myself, He could be an axe murderer!

He sent a bonkers voice note, 'I've got a plan that might work. Tomorrow, I'm dropping my daughter off at school, then I'm going to a funeral, but on the way back I was thinking I could pop by?' Adam had a strong London accent and enthusiasm in his voice. He sounded young and fit.

I thought, WTF?! I asked if he would be in the right frame of mind to meet me after a funeral.

He said he was good at 'handalling deaff' – hopefully he was better at that than at handling the English language. He asked, 'Is there anything you don't do?' It was reminiscent of the scene in *Pretty Women* where Julia Roberts tells Richard Gere's character, 'The only thing I don't do is kiss on the lips.' But I was not a prostitute! What the hell was I thinking? I didn't know this man from Adam (!) and he was essentially arranging to come over and fuck me after a funeral. But for some reason, I agreed to this ridiculous arrangement. I told him it wasn't my style and he said, 'I'm sorry, you just really turn me on and I can't wait to meet you.'

I was flattered, intrigued and a bit scared.

He went on, 'I want you to open the door in your underwear. I'm going to start by kissing you, then pull your knickers aside and start licking.'

I did put on my best underwear and suspenders, and

I shaved and bathed, but I also wore a dress I felt sexy in. I went outside to meet him rather than let him into my home immediately. I thought that if he looked nothing like his pictures then I could always run to one of my neighbours for help. But he was indeed unbelievably gorgeous. Probably the best-looking man I have ever come face to face with (except for Idris Elba). I was weak at the knees.

I (smoothly) said to him he was 'much better than his pics' and he just replied, 'Most girls say that.'

I took him upstairs and offered him a drink – he chose herbal tea. He wasted no time in grabbing hold of me and kissing me. He smelt amazing and he was so manly and tall, I almost had to stand on tiptoes to kiss him. He got a firm grip of my boobs and said he'd been looking forward to 'playing with these'.

He started to undress me and I helped him. I don't know where I got my confidence from. But before I knew it, I was standing in my lounge, completely naked in front of a stranger who had a rock-hard erection. He had an amazing six-pack and I almost wanted to take a photo of him, he was so handsome.

We moved to my bedroom and he suggested we sixty-nine. He was anything but lazy, saying throughout, 'I want to pleasure you, I want to make you beg for more.' It was erotic but robotic, mainly because there was no bond whatsoever as we didn't know each other.

After a semi-satisfying session, we lay there naked, sipping our herbal teas. It was bizarre. This unbelievably good-looking man, who looked like someone from an Athena poster from the '90s, was lying in my bed, drinking fennel tea, having rogered me senseless. He had a very simple command of the English language: 'How would you feel about me putting my penis inside you again some time?'

I just laughed it off, as I knew this was only ever going to be a one-night stand. But this was exactly what I said I didn't want. How did I get into this situation? I had been swept up in the excitement of it all. I had effectively provided an on-demand sexual transaction. All he had to do was send a few messages and pics and within twenty-four hours he'd been sucked, fucked *and* got a herbal tea! I felt pretty dirty and, despite using a condom, I was paranoid for a while and had a few visits to the sexual health clinic.

This was not safe on any level. But most of all, it did not make me feel great. I felt used. The thrill was outweighed by the dark, sordid side. I wasn't a slag, but this made me feel like one. Now I'm halfway through NOmenBER, I'm digging deep with my man detox and this is definitely a toxic incident I needed to confess and process. Going forward, I definitely don't need any more Adams in my life and don't want to be part of any more on-demand services.

ARTIST: Sia
TITLE: 'Cheap Thrills'
REASON: It's in the title!

Chapter 21

Just Convenient

It's 6 December and as with any detox, waves of emotions come unexpectedly and are at times extreme. I've made myself laugh, I've made myself cry, but today I'm having an angry day.

Why did I allow myself to be treated like that? Who the hell do those fuckers think they are? I bet they don't know how much they hurt me. Grrr...

There was a guy called Reece, who I met through work in my mid-twenties. He was a producer and I was the newsreader. Typical pleasantries were exchanged when we both started working at the radio station at the same time. I didn't think much of him at first as he was slightly scruffy and made little impression. Then we were sent on a new-starter course together. I didn't realise until I got the train to London and there he was, opposite me on a table seat. I was facing backwards (slightly annoying, all the way from Birmingham to London, but at least I had got a table). He peered over his gadget magazine and said, 'Hello.' We started off talking about work and what a 'funny old place' it was for both of us being new and not knowing anyone, but we soon got onto more juicy subjects like our interests, where we liked going out, music tastes and eventually relationships.

He was short but utterly gorgeous, a bit of a Tom Hardy lookalike. A bearded Tom Hardy with soft brown eyes and a winning smile. He wore slightly retro-looking clothes – corduroys, slim-fit checked shirts and Converse, but he was so good-looking that I didn't take too much notice of his attire. When we got to London neither of us knew where we were going and it was a gorgeous summer's day so we decided to navigate our way from King's Cross to Oxford Circus by foot. It wasn't a great distance, but far enough to build up a sweat and a thirst. We popped into a cafe and grabbed a drink. Despite the fact we had only really got to know each other on the two-hour train journey, he was quick to do that protective thing of holding his arm out in front on me to guard me from the traffic and he offered to buy my drink. I was very flattered and could feel myself being that giggly, red-faced girl, in the early stages of fancying someone.

The course was in an ordinary sort of boardroom with a giant whiteboard at the front, where we remained for duration of the day. We had to do all those typical 'Welcome to the company' exercises, with clichéd ice-breaker games to get to know our colleagues and company. The whole day I was aware of Reece's presence and kept thinking about our chats on the train, but also did that thing when you really like someone but pretend to totally ignore them for most of the day.

Just Convenient

We were to be put up in a lovely hotel in the centre of town for the night and were told at the end of the day's training that we were free to check in and freshen up before going out for welcome-drinks and dinner. I left independently, but just as I was struggling to swipe my entry card on the door to my room, Reece came up behind me. 'Are you having a blonde moment?'

I giggled and gently jabbed him on the shoulder, 'Shut up, it's just a bit fiddly.' We exchanged a few words about how the day's course had been pretty dull, but that it was still fun to be in London for the day. We arranged to meet back down in the lobby after showering.

It was so nice to get dressed into something more sexy for the evening as I had not prepared myself for meeting Reece on the train that morning and was feeling very drab with the corporate black trousers and shirt I'd worn all day. This was my chance to dress up a bit and potentially impress him with my evening look. We met in the hotel reception and he looked and smelt even more gorgeous. There's nothing better than a man straight out of the shower, their hair a bit wet, that smell of lovely, manly shower gel and the aftershave fresh on. He commented on how nice I looked in my summer dress, so I was glad I'd made the effort.

We met up with the rest of our course buddies and drank the night away, with free drink tokens issued to us by the company bosses. The whole night, I was keeping half an eye on whether Reece was noticing me across the dinner table and across the bar. I knew we were colleagues, so it probably wasn't a good idea to snog or anything but by the end of the night, we had drunk enough to be a bit more flirty. He was very quick to reach the stage of ripping the piss out of me.

When we left I just assumed he was heading into his room. But he took me completely by surprise and followed me. Before I had even worked out how to turn the light on, he grabbed me around my waist and started kissing me. It was so unexpected, but so sexy. He was very capable, holding me firmly but not forcefully. He pressed me up against the back of the hotel room door and pushed his fingers up the back of my head, through my hair. He slipped his hand up my skirt, creeping his way along my inner thigh and pushed my thong to the side. He slipped his fingers around the edge of my lips and felt his way inside of me.

Through the passionate kissing, he had made me very wet and I could soon feel his middle fingers caressing my clit. He said, 'You've wanted me to do this to you all day, haven't you?' I moaned back, 'Yes'. I really had wanted him to do that, more so than he possibly could have imagined. But while he had been flirty and showed an interest, I certainly didn't imagine anything would happen this fast.

We made our way onto the bed and carried on feeling our way around each other's bodies. He was a bit hesitant at times and before we got to the point of full nakedness and penetration, he uttered those heart-sinking words, 'I shouldn't really be doing this.' When I questioned him, he delivered the immortal line, 'Because I have a girlfriend back home.' I thought, *Whaaat*?! How have you spent all day chatting, flirting and now ending up in a hotel bedroom with me, snogging my face off, fingering me and letting me kiss you all over without mentioning this huge bit of information?

Just Convenient

He explained that he was in relationship with Jenny, who was older than him and although he loved her, they didn't really have much of a sex life. I battled with this in my head, but through my fuzzy haze (several wines) I convinced myself and him that 'This is just a bit of fun.' We got back to the excitement of him sucking my nipples and playing with my clit, while I moved my way down his toned stomach and started sucking his cock. A flash of guilt went through my head, as I thought to myself, This cock belongs to another woman, but he told me how good I was at using my tongue, so I continued. Our mutual tasting felt so carnal, as we had only just met, but we soon lost our inhibition thanks to the alcohol. The penetrative sex followed quickly, but after the build-up, he came almost immediately. I took it as a compliment, but at the same time thought it was pretty selfish. He took himself off to his own room to sleep. The next morning, we did that typical early-twenties thing, when you just act as if nothing had happened. The added insult was his lack of any interest in my well-being.

Ultimately, he had got what he wanted. He wasn't getting any sex at home and seized the opportunity with a girl on the train, after I showed a slither of interest. The thing was, I was twenty-four and immediately had feelings for him because we had slept with each other. That liaison in the hotel on the training course was just the start. At work over the next few months, I would take any opportunity to 'bump' into him while making tea or ask him for help in his producing role. I was smitten. I couldn't believe that Reece the 'hot producer' was interested in me. But looking back, if I'm brutally honest, he wasn't. He was still with his girlfriend the whole time. We just had stolen kisses on work nights out, when the company credit card was sat behind the bar, leading to a loss of inhibitions again and again and again.

He was never my boyfriend and he was never going to be but he was one of my first experiences of a work liaison. I had to learn to cope with the headiness of being professional on air, but my heart was pounding off air too whenever he was in the vicinity. And it didn't end there, as we both ended up leaving our jobs around the same time and I was overjoyed when Reece told me he was going to be moving to the same part of the southeast as me. The illegitimate liaisons continued but now that we didn't work together any more, we became more experimental.

One day we arranged to meet in a small village about halfway between our homes. He said no one would notice us in the car park of a country park and that we could find somewhere 'more secluded'. It was the middle of the summer and the ground was dry enough for us to sit on the grass, but we ended up stopping and kissing on a log. The kissing soon became heated. I could feel his hard-on pressing up against me and he lifted up my skirt and turned me round, to slip in from behind.

The problem was, this particular log was not quite as secluded as we first thought. Minutes into our intercourse, a dog whizzed past, indicating an owner was not far behind. The dog started sniffing around and we were quick to pull up our underwear. Once the dog walker had disappeared out of sight we got back to the matter in hand, but moved further towards a dip in the country park, which turned out to be a railway line. We were far away enough for it to be safe, but we were also close enough for a rush of blood to the head when a train went by. It was such a thrill, having sex outside, in the English countryside on a beautiful summer's day, with the risk of being caught and vibrations of trains zooming past periodically. It really was exhilarating.

On my way home, the buzz even affected my driving and I got caught by a speed camera. When the ticket came through weeks later I just thought to myself, He and that afternoon were worth it. After what turned into two years of sporadic sneaky meet-ups, I added him on Facebook. This was a risk, as it linked us on a public platform. I might even see pictures of him with his girlfriend for the first time and she might see me. But there was no reason for her to have any suspicions. Reece and I had been highly secretive. No one at work knew what was going on when we worked together and subsequent hook-ups had just been arranged over email. Then I received an email out of the blue: 'Hello, why have you added me on Facebook? You have my email. You are everywhere, aren't you? You fat bitch. You were just convenient at the time, don't contact me ever again.'

To this day, this is the most brutal message I have ever received, which is why I remember it so clearly. I crumpled into a heap on the lounge floor, sobbing uncontrollably into the carpet. What did I do to deserve that? We had mutually consented and as far I was concerned, enjoyed all of our sexual encounters. It had never been a regular thing, but over the course of two years, we must've met up a dozen times. I wasn't in love with him, but I was definitely infatuated. I was so hurt, I couldn't function normally for a few days, piecing together what had happened and tormenting myself by repeating his email in my head.

I couldn't help but wonder if it had been his girlfriend, finding out about me and sending an email from his account. But in a way it was clever because the guillotine nature of his email forced me to oblige. I didn't ever contact him again. Instead I just put the whole saga down to experience. I had played with fire and got my fingers burned. Reece was someone else's boyfriend, he was never going to leave her for me and I was just his bit of fun. It carried on far too long, but I was hooked on the thrill of the sneaking around with him.

I can look back and laugh now, as he was never very good at lasting more than five minutes, failed to ensure I was satisfied and he really didn't have much to boast about upstairs or downstairs. But it's amazing how good it feels to digest what happened with Reece, as that poison pen email has never left me.

ARTIST: Zero 7
TITLE: 'In The Waiting Line'
REASON: The lyrics describe wasting time and I was obsessed with this song during the time I was with Reece.

Chapter 22

(Anti)-Social Media

A friend of mine has been in touch today to tell me about massive row with her boyfriend. She was so inconsolable on the phone I could barely understand her. When I managed to calm her down and iron out exactly what the problem was, it turned out to be about Instagram.

Her boyfriend had 'by accident' let it slip that she didn't really 'look like' her Instagram or Tinder photos but quickly followed it up with. 'It's OK, 'cos I still fancy you.' Ouch!

But this is so true for so many of us, who portray an over-filtered, perfect image on social media and in dating profiles, but in the real world wear jogging pants, with no makeup and have a penchant for eating a whole bag of Doritos in one sitting.

This got me thinking about how the fake world of social media has crept up on us. Once upon a time I could hide behind the facade of having a 'good face for radio', as the saying goes. But over the course of time, having a social media profile has become part and parcel of working in the industry. From around 2002 listeners wanted to be able to see me on the radio station website and by 2007 they wanted to follow my profile on Facebook. In the early days I wrote my status updates in the third person – 'Verity is ... feeling the cold today.' It was so weird. This was followed by the explosion of Twitter and more recently, Instagram and Snapchat. This has allowed me to have both an on-air and an online presence. It allows for perfectly constructed, manicured images that present a certain persona for the public eye. This has also enabled a form of monitoring – or stalking.

When I was working for a radio station in central London, my biggest role at that point, I started to build up a profile. By this I mean they put posters on bus shelters promoting the radio show and I did interviews with big stars like the adorable Michael Bublé, which resulted in press coverage. It was a strange world of having more interaction with listeners while also getting a sense of loneliness and emptiness, as I didn't really *know* those people. I also couldn't really pick and choose the interaction I got. Sometimes it was highly complimentary, sometimes not – and sometimes it was creepy.

One day I started to receive beautiful, lavish bunches of flowers at work. The first time it happened, I had colleagues coming up to my desk asking, 'Who's the admirer?' but I dismissed the sender as a 'friendly listener'. I didn't really know. I just knew it was nice to receive the flowers at work. It happened a handful of times, and each time the flowers became more exquisite. They must have cost a fortune. They would come accompanied with a little card saying things like, 'Beautiful flowers for a beautiful lady'.

There was no public transport at 4 a.m. when I needed to get into work and I was picked up every day by a cab firm. I had a few regular drivers and I got to know them and their cars. One morning, I looked out of my window to see if the cab was there and it was absolutely chucking it down with rain. I didn't recognise the car or the driver. As I got into into the car, I said, 'Is this for Verity?' and in the rearview mirror the driver looked at me and with a thick eastern European accent replied, 'I finally get to meet you.'

I was unnerved but hurried into the cab to get out of the torrential rain. 'Are you OK to take me to my radio studios?' I said.

This slight, fair-haired man replied in broken English, 'It be my pleasure.' This was one of the most stomach-churning moments of my life. The car started moving and, as with a lot of cars, the doors clicked as they locked (*gulp*). I suddenly realised I was trapped in a car with a man who 'wanted to meet me', but what did that actually mean? I was dumbstruck and at first didn't say anything. As we approached the first set of traffic lights I thought to myself, I could just fling the door open and get out and run home. But it's actually pretty hard to open the door of a moving vehicle. So many thoughts were going through my head... Who *is* this man? Where has he come from? Why does he want to meet me? Where is he going to take me? Is he going to kill me?' Although I was ready to scream or cry, the fear and adrenaline became overwhelmingly calming. The journalist in me kicked in and I turned my mobile phone on to voice-record mode and started to talk to him.

ME: So, why did you want to meet me?

DRIVER:	I listen you on your radio programme for many time.
ME:	OK.
DRIVER:	I send you flowers.
ME:	[Heart sinks again – Oh, God] Why did you do that? [assertively]
DRVER:	I heard you say, you no husband, you single.
ME:	No, but I have a boyfriend.
DRIVER:	You sound lovely, you are lovely. I have dreamed meeting you.

I had the stark realisation that through the power of radio coupled with the transparency of social media, this man who had listened to me on my show and looked at me online felt like he knew me. He had listened to many conversations between me and my co-presenter about my antics. I have always been very candid about who I am, my relationship status, where I go, what I like etc. and it was only natural that people listening felt like they knew me. But on this occasion, being myself had backfired as this man wanted to act on my 'advances'. When I had jokingly said things like, 'I'm single and looking for love,' he had taken it as a personal invite. We continued our chat and I kept on recording on my phone:

ME:	So, how long have you been working as a cab driver?
DRIVER:	I just start.
ME:	What did you used to do?
DRIVER:	I work at flower market.

Oh, that's how he got those flowers.

ME: I see. So, why did you change to driving?
DRIVER: More money and I got to meet you.
ME: How did you get the job to pick me up?
DRIVER: I say, I know you.
ME: How do you know me?
DRIVER: I hear you every day. I see you Twitter.

Having listened to me on the radio, followed me on Twitter, he had now weaselled his way into a cab firm so he could pick me up. We continued to travel in the right direction, to my work on the normal route, and I got there on time. I ran to my desk and called the cab firm and asked what the hell was going on. They told me my follower was a new driver and they were sorry for any upset. I told my colleagues about it and they didn't really understand the severity of the situation. They just joked he would probably become my husband. Later that day the cab firm called me to confirm they had not carried out enough checks on this driver and he would 'no longer be working for them' and he had been 'dealt with'.

I wasn't really sure what this meant and was pretty nervous about heading home as this driver now knew where I lived. But it turned out to be fine. I can laugh at it now, as it feels almost like a cliché of a stalker story, in fact he even looked like the stalker in the Whitney Houston film *The Bodyguard*! I'm sure this driver never meant any harm and he simply wanted to meet me, but it felt like a very extreme way of going about it. This was a defining moment. This man didn't lay a finger on me but he still made me feel violated and vulnerable. It was an example of how naked social media can make you feel. You can use it to your advantage, by trying to build interest in your radio station or project, but you can't pick and choose who takes an interest. I'm certainly more cautious about who I interact with on (anti-)social media as a result.

ARTIST: The Police
TITLE: 'Every Breath You Take'
REASON: So synonymous with the story and
my time at the radio station.

Chapter 23

An Absolute Tool

Today I needed to do some Christmas shopping. While I toured around the shops with little direction, I found myself drifting into the lube section in a sexual health department. It's not something I've ever used, but maybe when I do get back into dating and meeting a good man it's something I should consider. When I think about how I have ended up in certain situations with men, I have to consider whether my behaviour encouraged the way I was treated. In fact, without meaning to be dramatic there have been a few dating landmines in recent times, which I need to get off my chest as part of my detox.

'Drill Man' was so named by my friends after I sent them his Bumble profile pic: a fair-haired, blue-eyed, muscular chap holding a huge, pneumatic drill. I was flattered that he had said, 'Yes' to my profile, as he appeared to be very good-looking. And no, I'm not kidding about the drill. He had nothing written but his photos depicted an active lifestyle, hanging off cliff-faces and showing off his muscles and physique. I guess I should've been more cynical about the lack of words. But as soon as I sent an innocuous message, his intentions became clear.

ME: Hi Cameron! How are you?

CAMERON: Oh hi! You have very big eyes!

ME: Thanks! I often get told that.

CAMERON: You seen from my pics I like to climb mountains?

ME: Yes! You seem very skilled at that? Tell me a bit more about yourself?

CAMERON: I'm a graphic designer from north London and I like mountains ;)

ME: Ha! How are you finding Bumble?

CAMERON: Yeah, it's al right.

ME: Had much success?

CAMERON: Loads!

ME: Wow, that's impressive! Why's that?

CAMERON: I've got a massive cock!

ME: All the boys say that!

CAMERON: Want to see it?

Oh, God, here we go again. Another cock-shot offer within the first few minutes of connecting.

ME: You must feel pretty confident with what you have to show me?

CAMERON: What's you number? I'll WhatsApp you a pic and you can decide. Speak to you soon, outside of Bumble!

An Absolute Tool

This is fairly typical conversation online. The red flags are there, including a stockpile of cock pics from his dating back-catalogue stored on his phone. He had no intention of meeting a girl to have a relationship with, but I was too intrigued not to take part in this stupid game. My mobile buzzed... And there it was – the most enormous cock, with pubes trimmed and his hand wrapped around the base of the shaft, making it appear more bulbous. Many penises are pretty ugly in a photo, but this one was kind of beautiful. He clearly had a gallery ready to go, for any willing Bumble maiden. I told him what I was thinking.

ME: I'm guessing that photo comes from your 'cock shot library'?

CAMERON: What do you mean? I just took that!

ME: Hmmm.

CAMERON: So what do I get in return?

ME: Erm, you need to work a bit harder than that!

CAMERON: Are you saying I need to do the whole first date and dinner thing?

ME: It would be nice to get to know you a bit better?!

CAMERON: OK, fair enough, but how about you send me a little teaser?

ME: All in good time.

CAMERON: I think I could really turn you on. I'd like to spend hours licking your clit.

ME: You certainly know how to get a girl excited.

CAMERON: You are exactly the kind of girl I like, great figure, blonde hair, beautiful eyes.

Over the next few days we continued to exchange messages and I really started to get a fanny twinge whenever I heard from him, even though he was effectively a digital romance. I only knew what he had told me and could only imagine what he looked like from the photos he had sent me. I liked what I had seen as he continued to send me cock shots. It got to the stage where my phone would buzz, my heart would zing and I would wish it was him, even though we had never met! I think it's all part of being a digital dating junkie. The highs that come with the attention from a complete stranger are addictive. He had very cleverly got me interested in him sexually from the outset and I wanted to meet him more than anything.

We arranged to meet in his neck of the woods, before heading off for some drinks. I got my hair blow-dried, bought a new dress and made sure my makeup was nicely done. I wore a black dress with fishnet stockings as we had previously discussed how stockings would turn him on. After making all the effort, I was praying he wasn't going to be perfidious. I packed a little overnight bag, as we had loosely arranged we would go for drinks and then head back to his house. All of the time, I could hear my friend Faye saying in my head, 'Don't sleep with him on the first date, make him wait.'

I got an Uber to the address he gave me and texted him on my way, so he was waiting outside his flat when I got there. I had a slight sinking feeling when I first clapped eyes on him, as he was not half as gorgeous in real life. He had a very weathered face and receding hairline that he had done a good job of masking in the Bumble profile photos. He was also not as tall as I'd hoped, but he was very muscular as he was in his climbing photos. He held my hand and took me straight up to his top-floor apartment, so I could 'drop off my stuff'. His apartment was nice, with impressive views across the London horizon, including the Gherkin and the Shard. As I was busy looking out of the penthouse window, I turned around to find Cameron with his trousers around his ankles and his massive cock starring back at me, like a real-life one-eyed monster. He was big, but also a bit red from where he had clearly been rubbing it, ready for me.

ME: Gosh, I didn't expect to see him so quickly.
CAMERON: Is he everything you'd hoped for?
ME: Er, yes, I guess so.
CAMERON: Come here and have a taste.
ME: Can I at least kiss you first?
CAMERON: Of course.

We started kissing and he was quick to try and reach up under my dress, but I moved his hand away.

ME: I thought we were going for drinks?
CAMERON: Yeah, we will but I just couldn't wait for
           you to sample the goods.
ME: Well, there's plenty of time for that.
           Where are we going?
CAMERON: [pulling his trousers back up] We're going
           to my best mate's fortieth.
ME: Er, OK! That's quite a big occasion for our
           first date.
CAMERON: I know, but I know you will fit in so well

	with my friends. You're a radio presenter, you can talk to anyone and I know my mates will love you.
ME:	[nervous] OK, cool, hopefully they don't mind me coming.
CAMERON:	Hopefully, you will be coming when we get home from the party as well!
ME:	You really have got one thing on your mind, haven't you?!
CAMERON:	You're a sexy lady. Of course I can't wait to have you in my bed.

It was all very flattering, but a tiny bit creepy at the same time. I wasn't really sure what I was signing up for, but we called a cab and headed to the party. It was a small affair, in a typical east London pub, full of bearded men in skinny jeans drinking real ale. Not really my scene, but Cameron was good at introducing me to his friends and I soon got talking to the wife of the birthday boy. She was absolutely beautiful and worked in TV, so we chatted about our careers and worked out we had a few mutual friends. She probed me about how long I had been 'seeing' Cameron and I just brushed it off with, 'Oh, not long.' It seemed too familiar for me to be at the party in the first place, never mind telling the wife of the birthday boy I was on a first date! She told me Cameron was a good guy, but 'never seemed to stick with the same girl for long'. This was insightful but not surprising.

Cameron kept me supplied with glasses of Prosecco and I returned the favour by buying a few bottles for the table. He left me to my own devices a lot, but periodically slid his hand across my bottom, whispering things like, 'I knew you'd get on great with my friends, can't wait to get inside that bottom later.' I giggled and blushed, thinking, You're *not* going in the back door.

By the end of the night I was *very* merry, and as soon as we got on our own in the back of the cab we started to ravage each other. Cameron was a enthusiastic kisser, especially with his tongue. Giving me a taste of what was to come with his cock. I was very accepting of his advances, as the drink had made us both very horny. He was quick to get me stripped off when we got back to his apartment.

He told me, 'I *knew* I'd love your body, plenty to grab hold of.'

Offended but drunk, I just carried on letting him explore my body. His body was not quite as muscly as I had expected. He had a lot of upper-body strength and a tight torso, but was very slim. He talked a lot about healthy eating and working out, so I was kind of relieved that he thought I was attractive when I was naked.

He was very keen to show me his giant, rock-hard penis and laid down, inviting me to 'taste it'. I licked up and down the shaft attempting to make it easier to get in my mouth, but it was a bit too big. Due to my drunken state, the sex was a bit of a blur, but I remember he was quick to get me to ride him, as I had told him in advance that was my favourite position. He said he was pleased about me wanting to go on top so he could look at me while I was orgasming. After some unsatisfactory pumping, he was quick to come all over me.

We soon passed out and he was snoring away next to

me. In the middle of the night after we'd both been asleep for a bit, I could feel him reaching round to hold me. He started by caressing my boobs, then my inner thigh and inside me, and soon started to massage my back door. I was still wet from where he had turned me on earlier, but when he was massaging my arsehole I soon became aware that I was wetter than I should be. Oh, God, what's happening? Had the copious amounts of Prosecco loosened my senses *and* my bowels? Was Cameron's rigorous massaging encouraging more than he had bargained for? This was horrendous.

I had never experienced anything like it. He hadn't even tried to put his penis inside my back door and this had happened. He didn't seem to notice, so I quickly got up and went to the loo to clean myself up. I turned on the stark bathroom light to discover runny brown stuff dribbling down my leg. It was a complete nightmare. I used the only toiletry product I could find in his sparse boy's bathroom – peppermint shower gel. I splashed some water from the sink and lathered it over my intimate area, which seconds later was tingling like fury. I realised I was not meant to use this particular minty shower gel directly on lady parts. It hurts again, just writing it. At least I was going to smell fresh down there. By the time I got back to the bedroom, Cameron had fallen fast asleep. Thank goodness.

The next morning, we woke up to sun streaming through the skylight. Cameron rolled over and kissed me but I felt absolutely disgusting. Morning breath, clammy body and the worst beer-fear from what had happened during the night.

He said, 'Would you like a cuppa?' As he got up to make

it, he yelled, 'Fuck me! Why are my sheets covered in shit?'

Oh God – I thought I had got away with it.

I just had to apologise and, after inspection of the brown stains on his cream sheets, he was pretty sweet about it. 'Oh, well, these things happen. Do you need a shower?' Although I had already had a wash, I leapt at the idea of having a proper shower.

I crept across his bedroom holding my low-slung boobs with one arm, trying to cover my fanny with my other hand. After all, Cameron was a complete stranger. I was absolutely mortified about 'poo-mageddon'. I thought I had managed to disguise the incident, but clearly it had been more of a disaster than first thought. I got out of the shower to discover him stripping his bed and bundling the load into the washing machine. I just kept apologising and saying I couldn't work out what had happened. I quickly got dressed and scarpered.

I had arranged to meet my girls for Sunday brunch that morning and I was so grateful I had them as my safety net after what I had been through. They could instantly tell I was in a bad way. I smelt OK, but I had clearly got last night's makeup on and a left-over blow-dry. They were, as ever, very complimentary about my appearance as I told them about the night before – but not all the gory details. There are some topics that need to be avoided at the brunch table, especially when ordering fresh, organic, brown juices. Ew...

The girls quizzed me over how I had got on with Drill Man, as they knew I had been on a date with him. Faye was quick to ask if I had 'done the deed', despite her advice not to. I just admitted that 'one thing led to another' and he had lived up to his Bumble profile persona by 'drilling' me. I continued to feel dreadful for the rest of the day. I cannot handle hangovers, especially when I've had so little sleep and a real-life nightmare between. I was not only feeling physically sick, my head was also full of regret.

This has to be one of my most toxic dating stories ever. I am really not proud of it and it's actually been very traumatic but also therapeutic writing it all down. In my eyes, dating apps have normalised promiscuity and have made it normal to groom someone, fuck them and fuck off – not acceptable. Cameron's motives were clear from the start, so I was not in any way surprised that I didn't hear from him again. For me, he was exactly the kind of online date I need to learn to avoid. From the word go our chat was sexual. Maybe this is what some women want. But I want a relationship and he definitely didn't. He wanted to fuck as many women as possible.

It was as if he had used a readymade formula in his approach. He was ribald from the outset and very quick to lure me with dirty photos of himself. Maybe a lot of women immediately tell him where to go. I can't deny it was fun for a time and the build-up to the date was exhilarating, but the end result was toxic and soulless. He didn't know that I had been through one of the most traumatic experiences of my life. I got home to search online, 'Why does alcohol affect your bowels?' and was comforted to discover I was not the first person to ask the internet.

This man detox is giving me answers to questions I have about myself but it is also revealing much about the wider dating world (and bodily functions). Cameron was an example of a man who portrayed himself with the best digitally enhanced and filtered photos he could create, as he didn't quite match up to his hunky drill photo. He was more haggard in real life and didn't offer quite the same effervescent personality he had tried to evoke. It scares me to think I've been caught up in a game in which so many people are attracting others with false pretences.

How far into a relationship do you have to get before you discover the real – unfiltered – version of someone? How much of the digital information you receive from a person is the real them? There can be a tendency to be more formal in messages. But there's also a liberating/dangerous tendency to be more outrageous than you would be in person. So much of the dirty chat I had with Cameron was in written form, rather than to my face. I should have questioned my own actions. There was an over-familiarity between us in the digital sphere that didn't transfer to the real world. I gained confidence from what we were saying to each other over messages that didn't match up to reality in the bedroom. He, too, must have been disappointed by the saggy boobs and blemished skin that had not been accurately depicted in my photos. We were fooling each other from the start. I should have been more true to myself when I was responding to his early messages about wanting his 'hard cock' when I didn't even know him. Ultimately, I shouldn't have jumped into bed on the first date with a complete stranger that I didn't know or like very much.

It all comes down to a desperation to be loved. We all want to be loved and I am holding my hands up here to say this was an occasion on which I tried to find a relationship through sex. If I had known it was going to be the one night of debauchery it turned out to be, I wouldn't have signed up for it. I often think I know what I'm doing but in hindsight (it's a great thing) I realise that it has been so bad for me. It was another notch on the bedpost (not to mention a stain on the sheets) I could have lived without.

It's easy put it down to experience, but there have been far too many experiences that have been detrimental and this was one of them. I'm not beating myself up here, I'm just being transparent. Yes, it's a vulgar/funny story to tell people, but I need to be good to myself and admit this is not me. It feels like I have been leading a double life: on the one hand I keep my professional profile squeaky clean, making sure I deliver exactly what's expected of me in my work, as a friend and a daughter and sister. But then there's a devilish side to me that succumbs to dirty one-night stands too many times and in the end it's futile. I need to make sure that whenever there's a temptation to head along this well-trodden path again, I remember dates like the one with Cameron. He might have portrayed himself as the handsome Drill Man but in fact I let him treat me like a complete tool.

ARTIST: Rag'n'Bone Man
TITLE: 'Human'
REASON: I'm only human!

Chapter 24

Burp Man

Even though I've spent my whole life surrounded by boys obsessed with sport, I still don't have much of a clue.

My dad and my brother love anything with a ball. My long-term boyfriend David was a cricket addict, and a few other men in my life have been into alternative sports like martial arts and cycling. The biggest sporting achievement of my life was cycling from Yosemite to San Francisco (330 kilometres) for a charity bike ride. It was one of the toughest and best achievements of my life, mentally and physically. I trained so hard for it and it helped me understand for the first time the passion that can drive you to fulfil a sporting goal.

Today I went to watch the rugby in the pub, far from the excitement of being in the stands but still a testosterone and beer-fuelled environment that was both passionate and rapturous. I have a few friends who have met the loves of their lives in these environments, but I've always found all eyes are on the screen until the final whistle. Men are not only focused on the ball but they lose all airs and graces – grunting, swearing, roaring, stomping, burping, farting and generally reverting back to their Neanderthal roots. But I get that there is something very liberating about letting out the 'real' man in the safety of the pub.

But while I am not against all these male traits, it can be hard to filter out the chaff at first glance when swiping left and right for a date. I was going through another stage on Tinder where I tried to avoid my usual type – manly, muscular, often black and handsome. Instead, I was swiping right on geeky-looking, intelligent types with witty repartee in their profile. I'd like to think the sheer weight of traffic in my dating app inbox allowed me to be a little bit more choosy. After Cameron I was keen to meet someone with a few more morals, someone less inclined to groom me, fuck me and disappear.

I thought Anthony fitted the 'nice' mould. He looked like Mr Muscle from the cleaning product adverts: slim build, glasses and he had a few photos with his cat. His profile was a really simple list suggesting he was smart but fun:

No kids
Never married
Animal lover (own two cats)
Very creative
Chilled
Ambitious
Chilled
Eat healthily

Burp Man

Keep fit

Voiceover artist

Let's see what happens

My weekend was fine, thanks (such a standard
opening gambit with online dating)

We matched and quickly started messaging each other:

ANTHONY: Hi Verity, great name! You must speak a
lot of truth!

ME: Ha! Yes. I'm very honest. How was your
weekend?

ANTHONY: Stop it!

ME: Just being cheeky!

ANTHONY: I like it. So what do you do?

ME: I work in radio.

ANTHONY: Yes, I saw your pic with a microphone
and assumed you were a broadcaster.

ME: What about you? Who do you do
voiceovers for?

ANTHONY: Loads of clients.

ME: Cool. Well, we may have some friends in
common as I know a few people who do
voiceovers.

ANTHONY: Yeah, maybe. Who/what are you looking
for?

ME: A good guy to have fun with, travel with
and ultimately settle down with.

ANTHONY: What do you like doing for fun?

ME: The usual: going out with friends,
cinema, theatre, weekends away, etc.

ANTHONY:	You like drinking?
ME:	Not excessively, but I don't mind a drink.
ANTHONY:	Can you burp?
ME:	I try to avoid it.
ANTHONY:	But can you properly belch?
ME:	Not on demand!
ANTHONY:	That's a shame.
ME:	Why?!
ANTHONY:	I find it a real turn on when a girl burps in my face.
ME:	Are you kidding?
ANTHONY:	No, the more guttural the burp is, the better. What about if you have a fizzy drink?
ME:	Noo!

And of course at this moment I had to delete him. What is wrong with men?! This was just disgusting and not what I signed up for when I started looking online for a man. It might not seem like a shocking request to some people, but it's not for me.

Friends have told me about worse requests. For instance, one friend met a guy who seemed perfectly normal, took her out for dinner, then the next date they ended up in a hotel. The thing was, he then asked her to poo on him. Again, this might be what some people are expecting from their dates, but I think it's pretty outrageous and doesn't lay the foundations for a loving relationship.

Chapter 25

Clean Pussy

Today I've decided to take advantage of my detox to cleanse myself mentally and physically, making sure I am in tip-top condition in the sexual health department.

I do my best to be careful, practise safe sex and get myself checked out regularly, but in the modern-day, disposable sex culture, I can never be too careful. It's always so embarrassing even entering a sexual health clinic with the great unwashed in a waiting room. I get to this clinic half an hour before the walk-in, to try and beat the queue, but I am still sixth in line – just a tiny insight into the demand on sexual health departments in the UK. I bet the dating app world has been a huge pressure on resources for these clinics.

I have not got any obvious symptoms, but I just want to get all my sexual disease tests done and make sure I am clear of anything nasty, as it has been a fairly busy year for me in the bedroom. I can't help but look around when I am in these places and feel uneasy – walls hung with posters and pamphlets offering advice on gonorrhea, chlamydia, HIV, bacterial vaginosis, genital warts, sepsis, pregnancy and terminations, etc. And then I look at the people around me and think, I wonder why *they* are here?

Today I can see a probably fairly typical crowd. There are two men holding hands, a woman who is heavily pregnant, a lady who looks like me (I catch her eye – thirty-nine, blonde, curly hair, looks a tiny bit sheepish), a few very young-looking girls and a lady who looks like she's in her seventies. She's perfectly entitled to have a healthy sex life, so I'm sure she's here for the same reason as me, to double-check she is 'clear'. Yet I can't help but imagine her story. Maybe she met a man on a fifty-plus dating site? Maybe she went for a younger man, someone who encouraged her to have unprotected sex? The possibilities are endless and it's always interesting to make up stories about people in my head, when I am people-watching and bored in a waiting room. Soon it will be my turn.

Maybe it's the British, stiff-upper-lip side of me, but it is never not humiliating putting my legs up in the air on stirrups while the poor nurse fiddles around to check everything is in order. I guess for her it's just like any job and she just gets used to seeing all shapes and sizes, but it's very odd to have a complete stranger (often with very cold hands and/or rubber gloves) feeling around my most intimate areas. I lie there thinking, Is it clean/tidy/healthy-looking compared to other women? There are also interrogating questions: 'What is your sexual orientation?' 'Have you had oral, vaginal and/or anal sex?' 'How many sexual partners have you had in the last few months?'

Clean Pussy

'Is he Caucasian, black, African...' etc. I realise they have to ask all these questions, but it seems such an invasion of privacy that by the time I leave, they know that I had carnal activity with a black man of African descent.

I remember there was one time I went to the GUM (genito-urinary medicine) clinic and, after going through all the necessary processes, I was told I had a clean bill of health (thankfully) and the nurse started asking about my job. I normally just say 'I work in the media' and keep it suitably vague. Unfortunately, she recognised my name and was quick to tell me she 'listened to the show every day'. I was mortified. I tried to style it out and just said, 'We all need to have these vital health checks!' Then she asked if she could have a photo with me. I nearly died! She had just seen all my intimate areas, felt inside me, asked me all about my sexual history and now she wanted a selfie with me! After that, very little embarrasses me.

Back to today and I'm looking around at all the contraceptives advertised on the walls. I can't help but think that the inventors of birth control have given recent generations so much choice. It's a blessing but also a curse. I have the coil, a preventative for pregnancy like the contraceptive pill, injection or implant, but these devices don't protect me against disease. It's very easy in the heat of the moment to think, Oh, I won't get pregnant, we don't need to use a condom. That is why clinics like the one I am at today are so busy.

I also think that my lack of sex education has a lot to answer for. There was next to nothing helpful taught at my all-girls school. We were shown some '60s science books with illustrations of male and female anatomy during biology, but I don't remember anything meaningful. In secondary school, there were some carrots handed out to place inside condoms during PSE (personal and social education) and everyone just rolled about laughing and the boys blew up the condoms into giant balloons. A load of people stole a stash of the condoms and discovered they were out of date as they were only meant to be used for demonstrative purposes.

The boys were also asked to leave the classroom when the menstrual cycle was discussed. Totally ridiculous! This meant a whole generation of boys at my school never understood anything about periods. Some men I have met in later life have so little understanding of the menstrual cycle, they thought that a girl used just one tampon for the whole cycle! It would have been so much more useful to have a decent sex education at school rather than learn about Jean-Claude visiting Lyon in our *Tricolore* French textbooks or simultaneous equations in maths. There were no tip-offs about the dangers of sexting, unprotected sex, contraception choices or how to cope when a man ghosts you.

While I get lost in my thoughts about poor sex education, I can hear the doctor call, 'Verity, is Verity here?' It's always so embarrassing, as I have enjoyed the anonymity in the waiting room. I don't have anything to hide, but it's a rude awakening.

DOCTOR: How can we help you today, Verity?
ME: I'm just here to get all of my STI checks
         done, for peace of mind.
DOCTOR: Do you have a new partner?

Clean Pussy

ME: Well, there have been a few over the last
           year. [red face]

DOCTOR: OK, well, let me ask who you have had
           unprotected sex with in the last three
           months?

ME: [counting in my head, James ... Ben ... Philip
           ...] Three.

DOCTOR: OK, well, let's get you on the couch and I
           will take a swab for gonorrhoea, chlamydia.
           If you'd like to go behind the curtain and
           take your trousers off and put your legs in
           the stirrups?

ME: [gets undressed and in position] Ready!
           [reminding me of shouting 'Readddyyy!'
           when I needed help getting my bottom
           wiped as a toddler]

DOCTOR: [holding a speculum, which for a split
           second reminds me of the pneumatic drill
           Cameron was holding in that Bumble
           profile photo] I'm just going to have a look
           at your cervix. Yes, there's the threads for
           your coil. And I'll just take a swab. That's it
           all done.

ME: That was all fairly painless.

DOCTOR: Yes, everything is in order. Just one thing,
           though.

ME: [heart sinks] Oh... right?

DOCTOR: If you use sex toys, make sure you clean
           them off before and after use.

ME: [Scarlet face, trying to remember if I had
           used my vibrator recently] OK, I will do.

Why on earth did she say that?! I was horrified! How did she know?! When I get home, I have a closer inspection of my intimate area. And there on my knickers is some fur! Some *cat* fur! It must have been from staying at my friend's house, where I left my clean clothes on the bed and the cat sat on the pile, making them furry. Maybe the doctor thought the cat had been sat on my vibrator?! I hadn't noticed that the black cat fur had stuck to my knickers and in turn stuck to my pussy. This was so humiliating and a massive lesson in making sure I have a clean pussy – in more ways than one!

ARTIST: Marvin Gaye
TITLE: 'Sexual Healing'
REASON: Relating to the mental healing that comes with knowing I am sexually 'clean'.

Chapter 26

Don't Do a Bog Brush

I'm halfway through the second month of my man detox and I must remember that being single at the age of thirty-nine has many perks.

Domestically, it can be blissful. From starfishing in bed at night (no one snoring next to me), watching what I want on TV and eating whatever I like (without judgement) through to keeping the house as tidy as I like. But maybe I have become too set in my ways in my years of independence and freedom. It is really important to me to live in a clean and tidy environment. That doesn't mean I don't want to share my space, but it's always music to my ears when a man says they're tidy. But there's always a fine line between wanting to help a man 'make a house a home' and upsetting the man-cave. I need to offload my instincts for neatness as part of my detox, as I must remember not to get too stuck in my ways as a singleton and inflict my standards and expectations when I do eventually get into a new relationship. As I always say, I'm ever the optimist that it will happen again soon, although my brother never lets me forget about a relationship that came to an abrupt end due to my domestic goddess tendencies.

I met Troy on Bumble and we matched after I'd let a good friend have a swipe on my behalf. She was in a long-term relationship and was thrilled to be playing what is essentially a game of snap on a dating app that matches potential suitors based on looks, name and age.

Troy was painfully shy, six-foot six-inches, had a massive mop of brown curly hair, a thick, bushy-brown (going grey) beard, intense brown eyes and very pale skin, and he was incredibly skinny. Not my type at all; in fact, not surprisingly, more my friend's hipster type. To me he looked like he needed a good bath, but he looked kind and seemed worth meeting. We went for cocktails at a very nice bar and the conversation flowed. He was very gentle and smelt divine.

We had very little in common, but we both appreciated the countryside. He lived in the middle of a remote town, where he had grown up. He was a scientist for a cosmetic company, more for a job that paid the bills than something that fulfilled his professional dreams. He loved anything '80s and sci-fi films, and was keen to introduce me to some of his favourites.

He invited me to his apartment for his 'legendary' spag bol. His gorgeous Georgian building was set in the middle of a quaint little town with a stream outside. It was totally idyllic. The apartment had high ceilings and grand bay windows with plenty of room for hundreds of books, DVDs, weird '80s memorabilia (including a hideous giant gremlin from the movie) and his vast collection of gaming equipment. There was a smell of damp as soon as I entered the place and he apologised. But I just said I knew what it was like living in an older property. The place was an absolute bachelor pad, with skid marks in the loo, years' worth of wiry pubes built up in all the corners of the bathroom floor, overflowing rubbish bins, sticky counter tops and stacks of washing-up in the kitchen, thick dust everywhere and piles of paperwork and stuff all over the place.

After his 'legendary' (very average) spag bol, we sat down to watch a thriller/horror he wanted me to see. Soon after the credits rolled he leant over, put his arm around me, started stroking my arm and eventually we kissed. He was unexpectedly confident when it came to taking the lead sexually. As he was otherwise a man of few words, he was hard to work out. So when he started nibbling my ear and telling me how much I turned him on, I was pleasantly surprised. After a couple of hours of snogging and touching each other, he wanted to 'get inside me', but I insisted we needed to know each other better, so I made my excuses and went home. Over a few dates we did get more frisky.

When I eventually got down and dirty with him properly, I discovered where his confidence was coming from. Despite his very slight frame his cock was nearly as long as he was tall! It was absolutely enormous and when I offered him a condom, he declined saying it wouldn't be big enough. The only thing was, as he was so skinny his pointy hip-bones dug into my inner thighs when I was on top and left my thighs bruised. Yes – that skinny! But he was very loving and caring as well as highly sexed. He got up the next day and made me breakfast in bed. And then we just carried on having sex until early afternoon. I was slightly icky about the fact he clearly hadn't 'had time' to wash his sheets – there were a number of dubious stains on the duvet covers.

After a couple of months of getting into our groove, with me going to stay at his a couple of times a week, he gave me a key to the apartment and space in his wardrobe to keep some stuff. It was all very easy between us and felt like we were heading towards living together properly. The problem was, even though I had subtly mentioned 'cleaning up a bit', he just didn't see the mess. One day when he was at work and I was off for the day I decided to surprise him by giving the apartment a spring-clean. I got up and went to the hardware store in the high street near his home and bought all the cleaning products I needed to spruce it up. He didn't even own a duster. I got some good music on and got to work.

I scrubbed the bathroom for hours, getting all the mildew out of the grooves of the tiles, wiping up all the pubes he'd trimmed and left on the floor. I dusted, vacuumed, wiped, tidied and made it look like new. I put away all of his gaming stuff which was strewn across the lounge floor. I also put away (hid) that ghastly giant gremlin which always felt like it was staring at us whenever we had sex. I bought some fresh flowers, nice smelling infusers and even a new bog brush, as his old one was vile – you get the gist. I didn't tell him I was doing any of this, I just completed my mission and left. He would come back to a lovely clean home after work.

That night I didn't hear from him, which I thought was quite unusual and a bit rude considering all the effort that had gone into making his apartment look spick and span. I messaged him but didn't hear back.

A few days later – it felt like an eternity – he messaged saying he had been really busy with work and hadn't had time to get back to me. But you can always see if people have been using WhatsApp and I knew there had been many occasions over the course of the week when I could see he was online, but he had chosen not to message me. We made a plan to meet up at the weekend and go for a walk. After a fairly cool reception, I could tell something was up, but I didn't want to press him on it as he was a very closed book at the best of times.

We stopped off at a lovely country pub on the way back and he went off to the bar, leaving his phone on the table in front of me. While he was getting the drinks, his phone buzzed and I happened to notice it was a message from 'Lisa POF'. My heart sank. I knew exactly what that meant. I couldn't read the message, but I knew instantly it was from a girl called Lisa from a dating service called Plenty Of Fish. After a few sips, I plucked up the courage to ask him who she was. His pupils dilated and face changed to an even whiter shade of pale. I had caught him red-handed. He was chatting to another girl, using another dating site, as he and I had met on Bumble. I was absolutely distraught and we returned to his flat where I sobbed and shouted at him, asking what was wrong with me and why he felt the need to find another girl from another dating app.

He was very unresponsive. He insisted he hadn't done

anything with Lisa and he was just chatting. He wouldn't admit anything was wrong and insisted he had loved being with me. I was devastated. Even though I had taken it slowly with him, making sure we had got to know each other over the course of a few dates before we slept together, and I had let him take the lead with what we did on the dates, I clearly still wasn't enough. I also thought the fact he'd opened up his home to me by giving me a key and letting me have space in his wardrobe meant things were progressing. He had also murmured about wanting to get married and have a family one day. We had a great sex life, I watched all his boring '80s movies and never bossed him about with anything. The whole thing left me flummoxed.

I told my brother about the situation to get a man's view and when I got to the spring-clean, he started laughing. He said, 'What exactly did you do when you tidied up his flat?' I reeled off the above about scrubbing, tidying (hiding the gremlin) and buying a new bog brush, and he started laughing even harder. My brother could not believe I had taken it upon myself to effectively transform Troy's own home and 'upset the man cave'. He thought it was nice of me and could understand why I would do it, as I was only trying to surprise Troy with a cleaner home. But when I revealed Troy had also been texting another girl from Plenty Of Fish, my brother said it was his way of finding another girl who didn't meddle with his stuff.

After many tears, I took my stuff and Troy and I parted company. To this day, I'm not really sure what went wrong. Did I fail to notice we were incompatible from the start? Could I have learnt to live with his smelly, soiled bedsheets and dirty house? Does it matter whether or not someone is a good person? Should I have accepted that he was talking to other girls from other dating sites while he was with me? Was he more of a predator that I cared to realise? Was Lisa POF one of many? Or was it simply because I hid his hideous gremlin? On reflection, things did move quite swiftly between us and I certainly made myself at home. I don't know if it was me upsetting the man-cave that drove him to another girl or whether she was on the scene the whole time. Whatever it was, he wasn't right for me. But even now, whenever I get anywhere near serious with a guy, my brother will still say: 'Don't do a bog brush'!

ARTIST: Chris Brown
TITLE: 'Loyal'
REASON: He wasn't loyal! Plus, I love this song.

Chapter 27

Clarity

M y friend always says to me, 'You can't help how you feel,' but I actually always want to challenge this, as I think there are things we can all do to help ourselves feel better.

I was going to call this chapter 'Failure' but as the day has passed I've realised it's not right. I was offline yesterday as I went to meet Ben. I had already texted him back and effectively opened up the conversation. I was visiting my auntie yesterday, and he works near there so I asked if he fancied meeting for a coffee. He texted me straight back to say he would fit around me and meet me whenever/ wherever. He messaged me later to confirm and asked if I fancied dinner instead. I agreed.

It was only a few weeks ago, at the start of my NOmenBER man detox that I said to Ben I couldn't see him any more, as he still lives with his ex and was showing no signs of committing to me long-term. And, of course, after only a few weeks, absolutely nothing has changed for him. But quite a lot has changed for me. By doing this detox I have started to get my head straight about what I want and where I have gone wrong with the men I have been with. From the outset, even when I was introduced to Ben, he made it clear that his number one priority in life is his daughter. This is an incredibly admirable quality and comes from a good place, as he wanted to be the best father possible. His own father wasn't great. I completely understand, but what I didn't realise until recently is that this meant there is no room for me.

What I had started to do on this man detox is look back at the time I shared with Ben through rose-tinted glasses. It was great, we had some lovely times together, we got on brilliantly, we had amazing sex and I love him. But looking back, there were lots of things that weren't right and I had started to gloss over them. When I arranged dinner last night, I felt that our meeting could be a test – I could see how I feel about him. I was strangely calm about it. The last time I saw him, we were still sleeping together, there were no issues and we just kissed each other goodbye. I spoke to him later and called things off.

Last night we hugged each other to say hello, which felt good rather than sad. He looked gorgeous and he was his usual smiley self. He was always a man of few words, but he was quite chatty about everything going on in his life and I was too. We talked about work, family, friends, etc. Then during the actual meal, we got on to the subject of 'us'.

I told him that I was breaking my own pact with myself, as I was trying to have time to get over him and 'reset' (I didn't use the words 'man detox' or tell him about my writing). I also told him I wanted to see him, as I was trying to listen to my instinct and I wanted to clear the air. For a brief moment I looked at his lips and thought about how amazing it was to kiss him, but it wasn't on my mind as much as I thought it would be. I told him that ignoring his message for a week didn't make me feel comfortable, as I wasn't being true to myself.

I chose French onion soup with stringy Gruyere cheese. This was a slight fail as I was battling with the cheese dangling out of my mouth as we discussed our relationship. I told him I felt sad that we couldn't be together properly but that I had to remember what I want. I (bravely) told him that I wanted to give myself the best possible chance of meeting a man who wants to get married and have a family with me. I had come to the realisation that this wasn't going to happen between us. He didn't disagree.

We also had a good chat about the fact it *is* possible for a man and woman to be friends. It just depends on the personalities of the man and the woman involved. He told me that he had a girl who he had grown up with and he was so fiercely close to her that everyone around them assumed they were lovers. But he said their relationship had always remained platonic. I reminded him that we too were friends first, before we started sleeping together. And maybe that was all we should have ever been. It was a bit of a *When Harry Met Sally* moment – minus the orgasm!

I also (again bravely) asked him if he had progressed with moving out of his shared accommodation, bearing in mind that this wasn't any of my business any more. He had told me while we were together that he wasn't happy with living with his ex, but had carried on doing so to keep his daughter happy. During our dinner he said he was 'going to tackle that soon'. But he also reiterated, 'The most important person in my life is my daughter.' And I think it was at this moment the fog started to clear for me. Ben's priority has and always will be his daughter. This is *never* going to change and that was fine, and it was the clarification that I needed. I want to be with a man who has time for me, as well as their kids (if they have them). I want to be with a man who wants to move heaven and Earth to be with me and not make me feel like second fiddle to anyone or anything. Ben can't/won't offer me this right now; it was as simple as that.

After an hour and a half together, he needed to go and pick up his daughter, so we parted company. It was perfectly nice to hug him and we said we'd catch up again soon. I don't know when this will be, but I am so glad the air has been cleared in case we see each other through our mutual friends over Christmas or at some other point in the future. I also feel like I've taken off the rose-tinted spectacles and given myself some clarity about where I am at. Even though I broke my own man-detox rules by meeting Ben, it enabled me to move forward. I had a little cry again today, but reminded myself it's OK to cry. I also realised that these weren't sad tears, just detox tears, as a means of flushing out the toxic feelings.

I think writing about my man detox has empowered me to say what I really want to say in real life too. Also, I've realised that things happen every day that influence how I feel and how I behave. For example, today a friend at work announced they are pregnant, which is nothing short of fabulous news. But I couldn't help but feel inwardly sad and wonder, When will it be my turn? But instead of relating these feelings to Ben, I was able to reason with myself that these feelings are more hormonal than emotional.

I can honestly say that meeting Ben for dinner last night has given me some closure. I'm not saying I'm never going to feel sad about him again, but I feel like I can't waste any more time with someone who doesn't want to be with me. I've taken off the rose-tinted glasses, the fog has cleared and I've got some clarity.

ARTIST: John Mayer
TITLE: 'Clarity'
REASON: The above!

Chapter 28

Submarines

I may have decided to stop talking to men, but it's been absolutely amazing how many of them have popped back up. They are the submarines. The men who you once met/dated/fucked, who disappeared without a trace and now pop back up again – when they are feeling lonely or need some attention. The men who flick back through their little black book (a.k.a. scroll through their old WhatsApp messages) at pivotal occasions in the calendar – their birthday, Christmas, New Year, Valentine's etc. Some men are so transparent, it hurts.

It's now December and a few of my cast-offs have been rearing their periscopes (ugly heads) after getting a bit lonely in the party season in the run up to Christmas.

Submariner 1

Take Jules, for example – he is unbelievable with his timings. He will regularly pop up at 3 a.m. with a 'Hello, sexy' message. Was that after a whole night of drinking, Jules? Or was that after a woman left you on your own for the night? I think the problem with him is we have never actually shagged, so there's still the thrill of the chase to be had with him. He is a classic: chased me, chased me, disappeared, chased me, chased me, disappeared, chased... and so it goes on!

We met during an interview when he was starring in a West End show. He was kind of a major deal at the time and acted very Billy Big Bollocks with me. I ended up interviewing him a few times in succession and we discovered we got on quite well. He then (smoothly) asked for my number, saying, 'It would be nice to get to know you better.' We ended up meeting up after I went to see him in his show one night and we drank the night away. It was fun, and we then went back to his house and had one of those disastrous drunken fumbles, where neither of us really knew what we were doing.

We woke up the next day, asking each other what we could remember. That awkward next morning with a stranger. You don't know each other well enough to snuggle up and spoon, and you have morning breath, but equally it's quite nice to have some contact as you are in the same bed. He was a bit cool with me in the morning and it turned out that he had a girlfriend. I would never have gone back to his house if I had known this, but he made it all feel very legitimate. When I quizzed him on it, he just said, 'She's my forever girlfriend, but I don't want to rip her clothes off... like I do with you.' Flattering as that was, I still felt a bit of female solidarity with the woman he supposedly called his girlfriend but didn't fancy. Why do men do that? Just stay with a woman so they can say they have a girlfriend? He almost made it sound like she knew what he was like and chose to ignore it. 'Bryony took me on knowing what I'm like, and I'm not saying she would approve of me being in bed with you, but she would also turn a blind eye.' I don't really understand why women do that either. It legitimises the behaviour. If you suspect your man is 'sharing his love', how can you just ignore it? Those turning-a-blind-eye women don't do any good for those of us singletons hoping for a genuine, long-lasting, monogamous relationship! They also make it OK for unsuspecting hussies like me to be taken advantage of by men who want their bit on the side.

For Jules this was just a way of life. And the way he got around retaliation is by not actually having penetrative sex, but doing everything else. Somehow, that was OK in his head! I met up with him on numerous occasions over the past ten years and we have always started off with a few harmless drinks in the friend zone, but it has also escalated to him fingering me under the table in a dark bar.

Once we met up in Camden, which can be pretty dingy at the best of times. It was absolutely pouring with rain, but we still sat outside this pub under the awnings and next to the heaters, so it was quite romantic. We were catching up for the first time in a while. Again, it started off very platonic, just two friends sharing a bottle of wine, but before we knew it we were snogging each other's faces off and because no one else was in the pub garden in the rain, I ended up sucking him off under the table. It was so naughty and animalistic, but of course it was fun and felt more harmless than full-blown sex.

These sorts of liaisons have been more detrimental than I care to admit. Yes, it was fun at the time, but ultimately Jules is exactly the kind of man I dread to end up with. A two-timing bastard who pretends he is happy in his relationship, so he can continue in the 'contented' home life when actually he's fucking a load of other people. Maybe Bryony is happy with a polyamorous relationship? Maybe she doesn't know all of the truth? Maybe she's at ease with his nefarious traits, as long as she has his heart, but not his sexual allegiance?

Loyalty is so important to me and yet I have had dealings with so many men who have about as much loyalty as a rabbit in springtime. Going forward, I think it's best to leave Jules, the submariner, in his murky waters.

Submariner 2

Someone else who has popped back up this month has been Simon. Yes, the flashy one who broke my heart after wining and dining me and then feigning an illness before dropping me like a ton of bricks and friend-zoning me. I haven't heard from him since the excruciating text, when I told him I 'missed his massive cock' (what an idiot). This was around nine months ago. Here we are in December and in true submariner style, he's popped back up again.

I assumed his reappearance was due to the frisky Christmas party season. Instead he's just become single again (rolls eyes). He said he was just getting in touch to say 'Hi', to see if I wanted to go for a drink, so I thought there was no harm in it, although I was well aware there was normally an ulterior motive. But having had some success in meeting up with Ben and clearing the fog with him, I decided it might be good to repeat this process with Simon.

We met at a pub local to me, which I was pleased about. But it turned out to be his local pub too, as he had moved even closer. He was dapper as always and looked at me with affection. After all, he had dumped me and moved on. I hadn't wanted it to end! But seeing him again made me realise I was not bowled over by his looks and that I had put him on a pedestal. We talked about what he had been up to and even though he had said to me he didn't want a relationship, he went on to be with someone for nine months! I also thought there had been some overlap between me and her, but I didn't bother raising that with him. It certainly made sense of why he had dropped me out of the blue.

He told me he had been dating a woman who was the same age as him and also had children the same age as his. The relationship had given him a good time for nine months, jetting off on various far-flung holidays. But when it came to the crunch and she wanted them to move in together, he wasn't interested and so they split up. So he got in touch with me. What a cheek! On the other hand it was nice to see him and catch up, as we didn't ever fall out. And as my friend Holly always says, 'They always come back.'

I was also pleased to meet up now that some time had passed. For a couple of months I hadn't been able to drive past a black Mercedes or his office on my route to the gym without getting slight palpitations. There was a time when he had a grip on my heart. However, after two months of clearing my head through my man detox, I have definitely reached a point where I am in a good headspace. And he could tell. He kept saying, 'You look really well V, you seem really happy.'

We had a nice night and I'm glad we met up as we had a good laugh. There's also been some closure, as he was very flirty but I just didn't feel the same about him. He also revealed he'd had a vasectomy eight years ago! Although he claimed he had told me that when we were dating, there was *no way* I would let my head get so involved with someone who had ruled out children. I also asked him about whether he had taken Viagra, as he was like a real-life Duracell bunny in the bedroom and even I couldn't quite keep up. He said he had never taken any in his life.

It was a funny set of circumstances, meeting up with a man who I thought had broken my heart. But once I had met up with him I was able to see he was just a cheeky, horny, early-forties divorcee who wanted a girlfriend, but not someone who was looking for marriage and kids, as he had only just done all that. If only he had been clear with me about that. Instead, I had built it up to be the start of a beautiful thing. Hindsight is a great thing, but if Simon taught me anything, it was to be crystal clear about what you want from the word go. I was trying to fit in with his desires, to be someone fun to play with. I was also trying to keep up with his insatiable sex drive, but even I couldn't do that!

ARTIST: Dua Lipa
TITLE: 'New Rules'
REASON: For the brilliant/accurate lyrics about waking up in bed with a man and if you're still under him you haven't got over him.

Chapter 29

The One That Got Away

I f I'm perfectly honest, I'm feeling a bit sorry for myself today.

A question I've been battling with over the last few days is, 'When it comes to men, have I made poor choices, or are the choices poor?' I am very trusting, verging on gullible and this is because I always like to see the best in people. As I hurtle towards completing two months of the man detox, I have been on a rollercoaster of emotions. The last time I wrote about Ben I was feeling quite empowered that I was doing the right thing by parking my feelings about him. But I've had a bit of delayed anger. In recent years I seem to have done a lot of licking my wounds and accepting friendships over relationships. Or was it me skewing the friendship?

A few years ago, a new guy started at my work and I was asked to show him the ropes. Richard was instantly likeable. He had floppy brown hair, a scruffy beard, kind eyes, brightly coloured, woollen jumpers with holes in, chinos and boat shoes. He was posh with a glint in his eye and the most charming, bumbly personality. He was always a bit flappy and uncertain about himself and his work. I enjoyed showing him how to do the job and we made an instant connection. We discovered we lived in the same area and had a mutual love of cycling. We quickly started to spend time together outside of work.

We would cycle, go for afternoon drinks and play Scrabble in our local, sitting next to an open fire, laughing until we cried about our terrible 'winning' words. I would invariably beat him, but that was partly due to the amount of beer, plus he was so kind I think he would let me win. He had recently come out of a long-term relationship with a feisty girl who had claimed assault. The police got involved and it turned very nasty. This was more to do with her attention-seeking than Richard's temper. He wouldn't hurt a fly. But he appeared to be very in love with her at one stage, almost enjoying her bossiness and erratic behaviour.

We started to share nights out with our own friendship groups. He fitted in beautifully with all of my amazing friends, just chatting away with them all and adoring them as much as me. I, too, met all his friends, some he'd had since boarding school and uni. He would always introduce me as 'my amazing friend V'. He would kiss the top of my head, play with my hair while nestling his six-foot self behind me, or kiss the back of my hand (like Prince Charming) all in front of his friends. So it wasn't long before they asked, 'V, what's going on with you two?' After a few months, we went to the work Christmas party and thanks to the free bar, we got annihilated. He came back to mine. I remember (despite the drunken haze) sitting on my slippery mustard leather sofa in my dodgy rented place in Chiswick and our bodies fell together. It had felt like the longest build-up to the longest kiss. He was so caressing and tender and it felt like fireworks going off in my head.

We moved to my bedroom, where we fumbled around and cuddled through the night, but we didn't actually have sex. He said, 'I don't want to ruin our friendship by having drunken sex.' I can remember the hum of that hangover the next day– it was definitely one of my worst ever. He got up and felt his way around my kitchen to make us both tea. We sat in bed, propped up with our tea (like an old married couple) and I asked him if we had slept together, as I couldn't remember a thing. He assured me, we had just spooned all night. In my head, there was a blur between feeling his hard cock press against my lower back in the night and the fact it hadn't gone inside me at any stage. I would've liked to have had sex, especially after so many months of build-up, but I was also grateful he hadn't taken advantage of me when I was so drunk.

Richard was nothing but a gentleman. He was always looking out for me, making me feel included in his life and helping make my life that little bit extra special. We carried on being the closest of friends, occasionally having drunken snogs. For example, there was another incredibly funny drunken night, where he decided he 'must' take me home after way too many beers. I was never a beer drinker, but he was a bad influence. It was a balmy summer's evening and he gave me a backy on his bike, as if we were teenagers. After wobbling in the 3 a.m. darkness around the empty streets of south London, with no one in sight, we eventually tumbled to the ground in fits of laughter. I remember laughing so hard, I actually let some wee out. It was magical. Instead of going back to mine, we went back to his and attempted to have sex, which was another fizzy-head moment for me, but it was more like two friends than two lovers. I remember lying in bed with him thinking I had fallen in love with my best friend.

We shared a bed on a number of occasions but we didn't ever really act like lovers. We were more like naughty teenagers who touched each other's 'parts'. He told me about his wild past while working in Amsterdam, where he had taken part in many vodka-induced threesomes. I felt like I couldn't really match up to these Dutch beauties he described, but instead was his real-life Bridget Jones. I was falling off the treadmill, making terrible meals for him (blue soup) and wearing unnecessarily short mini-skirts to get his attention at work. Also, having all those damsel-in-distress moments, when he would rescue me. He loved me and told me every day, 'You know I love you.'

The thing is, there is no better feeling than being in love. The trials and tribulations of life are so much easier to handle, which is why it means so much to find the right person. The problem was, Richard didn't love me – at least, not in the way that I loved him. I would get so excited about seeing him and my heart would skip a beat even when I saw his coat hanging on the back of his chair in the newsroom. I knew that meant he must be in the vicinity. Once I went to the train station when I knew he would probably be coming home from work just in case I bumped into him – and I did! It was the most magical moment of bliss; I had made an effort to dress up nicely, do my hair and makeup and then 'stumble' across him, looking my best. He had no idea I had engineered the situation just to steal another moment with him, but I started to believe this meant it was fate and the start of a beautiful romance.

I got to know all of his friends and family just as if I was his girlfriend. I pushed aside the fact he wasn't offering me a real-deal relationship. Instead, I woke up every day making sure I looked good for him at work. For eighteen months he gave me everything I wanted from a man – except the title 'boyfriend'. Then he broke the news that he was off to work in Cambodia. My heart split in two and my face must have revealed my heartbreak but, through gritted teeth, I beamed with excitement for him and congratulated him on the incredible news. I knew this was the end of 'us'. He was going to go off into the sunset, to start a new life and inevitably meet his princess.

We gave him an amazing send-off with a great party attended by all 'our' friends, his insisting I stayed in touch with them, as they were now my friends too. It was the March of that year when he flew off and I honestly felt like my world had been torn apart. The pain in my heart was indescribable: it felt as if it was physically cracking. I had been broken-hearted before, but this was a double whammy. I remember standing in the shower one day, with tears streaming down my face, whacking the shower wall with my fist, not caring that I was leaving my hand black and blue. I was so hurt, I was so angry and didn't know what to do with myself.

I drove to work and could barely see the road for the tears streaming down my face. I had not only lost my best friend but I had spent eighteen months dreaming – I thought we were building solid foundations for a lifelong relationship. His departure was a sledgehammer smashing through those dreams. He had gone off to discover a whole new life, but I was left behind with a Grand Canyon-sized hole in mine.

Over just a matter of weeks our contact dropped away. Having been promised regular Facetimes, I knew this wouldn't last, especially when he met someone new. It wasn't long before photos of him appeared on Facebook with a stunning girl. My heart shattered all over again. All of his school chums commented, 'Who's the hottie – you are punching there, mate.' This gorgeous girl was Rachel. She was ten years younger than Richard and had swooped in almost within minutes of him arriving at his Cambodian office. It wasn't long before the photos on Facebook suggested they more than just friends. I inevitably tormented myself by cyber-stalking her, slicing up my heart like chopped liver by looking at how utterly beautiful and skinny she was, repeating in my head, Why her, not me?

Richard returned to the UK four months later, in July, for the wedding of one of his best friends. John and Kate had become my friends too, thanks to Richard introducing me. We were all invited to the ceremony in Suffolk and Richard suggested that we team up and share a B&B. This filled me with excitement. I thought that this was another chance for me to 'sleep with' Richard and convince him to be with me. What I didn't realise until we checked in was that Richard's 'very keen' friend Max was also joining us, 'kipping on the floor'.

After a fabulous time at the wedding, all three of us piled into the tiny bedroom, where there was a double bed and a single bed. I totally assumed that it would be Richard and I in the double and Max on the single. But after a lot of ribbing from Max about Richard's new 'punching-above-his weight-fucking-stunner' girlfriend, it turned out he wasn't even available to share a bed with me any more. I ended up being forced to share a bed with Max, who 'only ever' sleeps naked and spent the whole night trying to press up behind me with his semi. How did this happen? How on earth did I end up in a bed with Max and not Richard? I didn't fancy him whatsoever. I knew I couldn't be with Richard either, but I still wanted to be in bed with him. Just one last time.

I didn't really get a chance to talk to Richard on my own during his visit. We did, however, make a plan, that I should visit him in Cambodia for New Year, as part of a trip I was going to make to Australia. This was a date in the diary and something to look forward to. Between July and the end of the year my heart started to mend itself. It probably helped that I hardly heard from Richard. He was busy building his new relationship with Rachel. By the time I got to Cambodia they were living together.

I had obviously never met her or spoken to her and I was so nervous about it. Richard met me from the airport and it was fantastic to see him again. When we arrived at his house, Rachel gave me a very warm welcome with some Cambodian gifts. Although I feared I would hate her, she was lovely and I couldn't help but like her. She was absolutely beautiful, very young, immaculately dressed and permanently topping up her lipgloss. She was also incredibly kind-hearted and the main thing was she made Richard exceedingly happy. It was great to stay, except I had to listen to them having wild sex next door at night and in the mornings, which was pretty galling. But they treated me like a queen and we had enormous fun visiting all the amazing sights of Cambodia.

In what turned into a few years of wedding following wedding following wedding, the moment came when Richard and Rachel decided to tie the knot. The invitation arrived on my doormat giving details of a reception in Beijing and I thought, Yes, I would love to go to China for a wedding. They also asked me if I would do a reading at the ceremony. Of course, I obliged. To this day I think it was pretty brave of me, especially as the reading was about two dinosaurs falling in love! Deep in my heart I wished it was me walking up the aisle with Richard, but I was still incredibly happy for them and honoured to play an important part in their special day.

As I write this, almost two months into my man detox, I ponder, 'Have I made poor choices, or are the choices poor?' But when I think about some of those choices, they have been amazing. Richard was never really my boyfriend, but I still loved him. In fact, I will always love him, but only in the platonic sense. We are still friends now and I am still very close to his friends and family. Essentially, I fell in love with my best friend and although I did choose him, he didn't choose me. Going forward, I need to remember that although it would be nice to be best friends with the person I eventually fall in love with, I need to choose the person who chooses me.

ARTIST: Randy Newman
TITLE: 'You've Got a Friend in Me'
REASON: One of my favourite songs and it says it all!

Chapter 30

Oh My Dayz

Watching the TV is not something I bother with very often, due to lack of time and my terrible attention span. But I have been better at chilling out while I've been doing this man detox. While I was watching TV last night, a guy I once had a dalliance with popped up on the screen.

I often get asked, 'Aren't there any nice men at your work?' Work can be such a good place to meet someone as you see them every day. They also see you in your professional capacity and there's something very naughty about presenting a corporate persona one minute and getting naked with them the next. However, if you do sleep with someone at work, there's always the risk it can turn sour and there's a reason 'don't poke the payroll' is a well-used saying.

When I first met the man who graced my TV again last night, I had been gradually working my way up the career ladder. I had almost reached a position I'd always wanted, thanks to an encouraging boss and her understanding that I also needed to work in another office each week. The other office was more exciting as there were so many more hot men. I used to get picked up by cab as there was no public transport at the crack of dawn when I started, and I did my makeup on the way, giving me a few more minutes in bed. A guy called Steve did the same job as me and he always greeted me with a big smile and hugs whenever I worked in his office. His peers would rib him about the fact I got the biggest reception compared to the other women in the office but I just put it down to being the new girl.

I was invited to Christmas parties in each office that year, which was so exciting. I knew that Steve would be at one and this was our chance to get to know each other socially. There was lots of banter about mistletoe and he promised me a dance when we heard the party was at a nightclub. I planned my outfit meticulously, bought a new party dress and shoes, had my hair styled and got my makeup done professionally. I felt amazing. I remember walking into the party, on my own, adrenaline pumping and a head full of questions: What if Steve doesn't notice me? What if no one talks to me? What if I get too drunk and say the wrong thing? What if I fall over? In other words, all the normal Christmas party drama!

The dark and dingy nightclub smelt of stale beer and the music was thumping. It was half-empty, but fortunately I bumped straight into one of the sweet girls from admin who had always been really friendly whenever I'd seen her at the other office. We went to take advantage of the free bar and got on it, with shots. Everyone looked gorgeous in their Christmas attire, with many people (including men) looking unrecognisable. One of those men was Steve, who had rolled out a snazzy suit and white shirt and tie for the occasion. He acted very cool, but still came swaggering up to me, 'You scrub up well, Verity.' He cheekily offered to 'buy' me a drink, even though I knew the drinks were being covered by the company credit card.

We chatted, drank, chatted, drank, chatted... and before I knew it, Steve had taken me to a booth for a drunken snog. He had pursued me for some time at work and I was pretty uncertain about him at first, as it seemed he was a bit of a notorious stud in the office. We stayed out of sight for most of the night and then he suggested we go back to mine. I went to get my coat and another girl, who I didn't know very well, gave me a knowing look. She sidled up and whispered, 'You know Steve is bad news, don't you?' I asked her what she meant. 'I've been there – and so have half the office.' Ouch! This wasn't the most shocking news I'd ever heard, although it still made me feel pretty cheap, but nevertheless I ended up leaving with him. He might have sampled half the office but, as far as I was concerned, I was the one he had selected to be with for now (or for tonight, at least).

Steve was all over me in the cab. He was very small, but strong, with bulky arms and a defined six-pack. He was gorgeous, but had always lived in the shadow of Harry, another office stud. He asked me over and over again, 'Are you sure you don't want Harry?' I assured Steve I wouldn't be taking him home if I preferred Harry. Steve had very much marked his territory with me, almost like a cat spraying around a room. Even if I did fancy Harry, I was never going to get anywhere near him with Steve always being around.

We got very passionate in the back of the cab (poor driver). Steve's hand was up my skirt and on my boobs and I was feeling his hard-on through his trousers. As soon as we slammed my front door shut, the snogging resumed and the clothes started to come off. He was rampant. He was so strong and we left a trail of party clothes and underwear all the way to my bedroom. He lifted me onto the bed with my legs wrapped around his hips. It was so exciting to have him in my house after all the chasing at work. He attempted to finger me and discovered I was already wet, whispering, 'You're soaking, I love it.' He was a bit too rough with his hand, so I moved away and went down on him. He said he didn't really like it, as an ex-girlfriend had made him paranoid about never coming in her mouth. It made me think we were better off getting on with the deed. He asked me if I had condoms and I realised the nearest were in the top of my wardrobe in my medical box. I had to break proceedings, grab a chair and reach up. Smooth! I should've been more prepared.

Despite the embarrassment, I didn't care as it was more important for me to practise safe sex, especially if his reputation was anything to go by. He was very acrobatic, flinging me around the bed and asking repeatedly, 'Have you come?' I just thought to myself, If you have to ask, you've probably got your answer.

Before I knew it, he was shouting, 'I'm gonna come, I'm gonna come...' and then at the euphoric orgasm moment he exclaimed, 'Oh my dayzzz, oh my dayz, oh my dayz...' I'd never heard that one before! I was ready to laugh out loud.

It's so funny how men (and maybe women, I wouldn't know) make such different noises and shout things in the heat of the moment. Whether they're screaming like a girl or grunting like a pig, that first time you sleep with someone can often be quite funny or awkward.

I later told a group of girlfriends about what he'd shouted. This started a conversation about what men say or do at the moment of climax. So many of us, men and women, don't even realise we are doing it. I remember a girl I lived with once shouting, 'This is *your* pussy!' really loudly as an estate agent walked through the house. Another friend said her husband shouted, 'Take my baby gravy!' in the heat of the moment. So many men I have known have squealed like pigs or roared like tigers. We definitely all have a sex face when we are reaching ecstasy and Steve has always been known to my friends as 'Oh My Dayz'.

We cuddled for a bit, but then Steve decided he wanted to get home. This was a big disappointment, but I acted like I was cool with it. This wasn't exactly what I had in mind. But it was classic animal behaviour – the months of chase at work, the build-up at the party and then, bingo, he got what he wanted.

I messaged him, 'Thanks for a great night,' but there was little contact after that. The problem was that we worked together. I was going to see him over and over again whenever I worked at his office. And I did. He would acknowledge me from then on but acted like nothing had ever happened. He certainly didn't behave the way he did before the Christmas party. There was no challenge for him any more. I was just another conquest in the office. The girl who'd warned me about him had been right.

Man Detox

By Valentine's Day the following year I was working in Steve's office permanently. I remember sitting at my desk and a cupcake decorated with a rose landed on it. There had been some dirty banter between Steve and I about him 'getting inside my rose'. I was red-faced immediately, but also flattered. I could see there was a note with it, 'With love from Steve'. The thing was, it wasn't addressed to me. I sat opposite another girl who was actually married with kids. The cupcake was for her.

Why would Steve do that? Why would he torment me by giving another girl, who wasn't even available, a Valentine's cupcake with a rose on it? I got choked up, unable to hide my upset. The intended recipient put her arm around me and asked if I was OK. Even though Steve had sworn me to secrecy about our liaison, I was mortified and blurted out what he had done. It was his blatant dismissal, even though I had previously let him 'inside my rose'. I had been very messed around by Steve but I still wanted him. You always want what you can't have.

I was quick to forget about the cake incident and there were a few more encounters between the pair of us. I was mad about him. It was so hard seeing him at work every day, knowing what had happened. Each time he did get me he dropped me immediately afterwards but I stupidly went back for more. There was also an occasion when he snuck up behind me in the kitchen. No one was around as it was early in the morning. He started kissing the back of my neck, lifted up my dress, reached his hand round and started fingering me while I was making the tea. This kind of stolen moment came along fairly regularly over the course of a few years.

They say love is a drug and Steve was definitely one I was hooked on for a while. I feel absolutely nothing for him now. We definitely had fun, but would I do it all again? Hindsight is a great thing and I was younger and more frivolous than I am now. Those stolen moments aren't exactly something to tell the grandkids about, but they happened. Rather than dwelling on the fact I was messed around and used by the office love rat, I think he played a part in me improving my self-respect. I would think twice about getting involved with someone at work these days.

He never ever let me forget about the 'medical box incident'. But seeing him pop up on the TV last night, I was able to just smile to myself and think, Oh, there's Oh My Dayz... your loss, buddy.

ARTIST: Pitbull featuring Ne-Yo, Afrojack, Nayer
TITLE: 'Give Me Everything'
REASON: It was the song of the moment at that Christmas party.

Chapter 31

Textual Intercourse

The thing about having sex is that if you have it all the time, you don't think about it, but when you stop yourself from having any, you think about little else.

Now I often look at people around me in the street or at work and think, I wonder when *you* last had sex? I genuinely believe that some people are born more sexually charged than others. My earliest memories of wanting a boy date back to when I really, really wanted Oscar Greenhouse to borrow my pencil sharpener at junior school. I must have been around eight or nine years old and I didn't understand the feelings, but I knew that it was only him that I wanted to lend my pencil sharpener to. I would give myself any available opportunity to be 'that girl' he chose to talk to.

In the playground at break, we would play kiss-and-chase and even have pretend weddings behind the PE shed, where we would take it in turns to let a boy and a girl 'make a wedding'. This would just involve the boy and girl (Oscar and me) sneaking behind the PE shed and staring at either other and giggling for a few minutes before going back to the friends, watching out for the teacher, and declaring, 'We are married.'

It's funny how this sneaking around authority continued into my adulthood. Maybe I have been a rebel without a cause since the age of eight, or maybe all of this is just natural exploration of the opposite sex. As Danny DeVito once told me during an interview, 'Verity, we are animals and we like rubbing up against each other.' This was in response to me giving him a pretty inappropriate hug instead of a handshake. I apologised, but I told him I had felt compelled to do so as he's so famous he looks familiar and it felt completely natural. Fortunately he didn't mind and understood that sometimes you just want to hug someone. My point is that our animal instinct makes us feel compelled to touch another person and sometimes it's hard to resist. Of course, this is not how civil society works, but there have been occasions when I have felt so compelled to touch someone that the next best thing has been telling them.

When I first started out as a broadcast journalist, I was thrust into established newsrooms full of people who had been there since the beginning of time. It was daunting being the newbie, but it was also nice being given attention by those who were clearly bored with all the other people who had worked there for so long.

Will Parker had been at the radio station a long time because he was born and bred in the area. He took an instant interest in me, telling me most days I looked nice and asking me how I was getting on with the new job. At times I was having to ignore his eyes burning through the back of my head, as I was new to the job and had much to do that required concentration. But once I started to feel more at home with the equipment and become more confident, I was able to take a bit more notice. He told me he was married with two children and I knew there was no point in even talking to him in a flirty manner. One day a message popped up on the instant messaging system. I hadn't used it before and scrambled around with the mouse for a few minutes trying to work out how to respond to his words flashing on the menu bar at the top, 'How do you like your coffee?'

It was funny how this instantly made my heart pound. The warm greetings he'd offered in person were transferred to the more liberating arena of digital messaging. I replied with an instinctive, 'Strong and black, like my men!'

His perfectly innocuous message had allowed for cheeky banter in return from me. I knew he didn't really care how I liked my coffee. Will was the opposite of strong and black. He was tall, of average build and had mousy brown hair and glasses. He had lovely blue eyes, a big nose and a cheeky smile. He wasn't really good-looking, but due to his flirty nature he had stood out. And this coffee chat soon escalated into more risqué banter. 'What do you like these strong, black men to do to you?

I was in the middle of editing a radio package and my deadline was only two hours away, so I really didn't have time for cyberspace flirting. But after a couple of minutes, I batted back an innocent response, 'I like a man to make me coffee, of course ;) ' And then a few minutes later when he didn't reply, I thought I would spice things up. 'Make me coffee... naked'.

Will replied, 'Oh, right... what would you be wearing?' He had been taking a particular interest in a pair of knee boots I had been wearing to work. They weren't particularly sexy but I think by the very nature of being knee-high, he was letting his bored-at-work mind run away with him.

'I would wear my knee-high boots...'

'Anything else?'

'Nope.'

'I would pay to see that.'

I could see over the top of my desktop computer that he was smirking at his screen. The whole time I was thinking, I have so much work to do, I really hope no one walks past either of our computer screens and spies these messages. I then had a moment of panic and thought I'd better park the conversation. 'Aren't you a happily married man?'

After a few minutes of him pretending to be busy, he replied, 'Well, yes, I'm married.' So he was tied down, but not necessarily happy.

ME:	Well, you shouldn't be flirting with me then!
WILL:	It's only banter.
ME:	You are still naughty.
WILL:	You wouldn't believe how naughty! You have got me excited...
ME:	You will have to let your imagination run wild later, as I have too much to do right now. Bye!
WILL:	OK, talk about stopping me in my stride. But OK, you get on with your work, young lady.

Textual Intercourse

I wonder if it was because I wasn't allowed to be talking to Will that our chat was all the more tantalising. There we were at work, both hurtling towards deadlines but instead distracting each other with ridiculous, flirty instant message chat. I felt like I had a devil and an angel sat on either shoulder:

ANGEL: He's married. You shouldn't be doing this.

DEVIL: You weren't really doing anything wrong. It's just words.

ANGEL: Just walk away now. How would you feel if this was your husband?

DEVIL: You aren't going to act on these words, they are just words. It's just a little crush.

A few hours later, Will saw me go in the studio and do the piece I had been working towards. When I came out of the studio he figured I had finished what I was doing. I came back to my desk and saw a new message flashing at the top of my screen.

WILL: Shall we carry on with our coffee break?

ME: You are so naughty!

WILL: You have no idea.

ME: I think I get the idea.

WILL: Have you ever had a wank race?

ME: Errr... not at work!!!

I could feel my face go scarlet and was desperately trying to continue with pretending to work at the same time.

WILL: I want to explore what will turn you on.

ME: That sounds intriguing.

WILL: OK, how about this...

At that exact moment, my boss swung by my desk. 'How did your two-way go, Verity?' My heart hopped into my mouth as I wondered how long it taken him to sidle up to my desk. Did he see my messages with Will?

Dying inside, I told him, 'Yeah, it went really well, thanks. I was so glad I managed to get a couple of voices on the story...' While quickly trying to make out I was completely enthralled with what I had been doing, I was praying that Will hadn't seen my boss peer over my shoulder. Any minute now, he was highly likely to send me a dirty message. My boss told me he was pleased with what I had done and thankfully walked off just as another note from Will popped up. My heart was pounding in time with the flashing message.

'And they're off... I would very much like to gently run my fingertips over your pussy lips, tease out the wetness, then put my fingers in your mouth and kiss you deeply.'

I pulled back from my computer, leaned back in my seat and gripped my hair. This was a serious turn-on. Where the fuck had this come from? He was just the dude from the sports desk who had occasionally told me I looked nice. Here I was, ducking and diving with my boss while this unexpectedly filthy man was sending me very erotic messages. I sat there for a second and contemplated if I should reply. I typed slowly, 'Such a turn-on. I want you to taste me. I get very wet. I will probably get very wet just kissing you. I haven't even kissed you and I can feel myself getting wet.' As I pressed the send button, I could feel my heart in my mouth. I thought, Fuuuck! WHAT AM I DOING? But it was exciting, it was naughty.

WILL: Like the thought of you sitting there getting wet, I had no idea.

ME: Have I said too much?

WILL: Err, no! Tell me more?

ME: I would love to spend some time exploring your cock with my tongue.

WILL: You can spend as much time as you like exploring my cock.

ME: Have you got much to explore?!

WILL: Well, I've never had any complaints...

ME: Ha!

WILL: You happy with a hoodless cobra?

ME: What?!

WILL: I have been circumcised.

ME: Woah! That's a lot of information!!

WILL: Sorry, but I wanted to paint a true picture.

ME: I went out with a Jewish guy for five years and he had the 'lid off' so, yes, that's fine.

WILL: Phew. I want to be between your legs, lapping up your wetness, making you come with my tongue.

ME: You have great lips, which I can't stop looking at. I can feel the wetness seeping down my leg now. Just the thought of your tongue getting deep inside me is making my clit tingle and my nipples erect.

WILL: When we were in the kitchen earlier, I realised

how much I wanted to kiss you. I didn't think
you would be interested.

ME: Ditto.

WILL: What?! You didn't think I would want to kiss
you? I thought you liked black men?

ME: Let's remember you are a married man who
works in my newsroom.

WILL: You're right, but this is fun, right?

ME: Yes, but I want you to know that I do feel guilty.

WILL: I want to push your legs apart so I can lick you
as deep as possible. Maybe let my tongue go
lower, tease your arse a bit. Reach up and play
with your nipples.

ME: OK, you're making me want to run to the ladies
loo and finish this 'race'.

WILL: You have no idea what you're doing to me right
now as well.

I got up and went to the loo, mainly because I didn't want
to carry on with this filthy chat on a work computer. What
if someone from IT could see what we were saying to each
other?! This was totally wrong on every level, but it was so
exciting at the same time. In the loo I bumped into Kelly
from the record library, who soon brought me back down
to earth talking about the weather and how it was going to
be freezing on her bus journey home. Zzz.

I couldn't have felt less sexy inside a work toilet
cubicle with Kelly talking at me through the cubicle.
I was not going to actually touch myself intimately in
these circumstances. This was a stark reminder of the
ridiculousness of the situation. There I was, doing my job

as a broadcast journalist, supposedly concentrating on my story for the day, but also creating a naughty fantasy with Will from the sports desk. I got back to my desk to find another dirty outpouring was arriving.

WILL: Where did you go? Did I offend you? I hope not. I have just been thinking about how good you would taste.

ME: Stop it! What if Tony from IT can see our conversations?! I would die. Someone once told me that emails are like a postcard, anyone can see it. I'm not sure how it works with instant messenger.

WILL: Nah, it'll be fine. Things were just getting good...

ME: I get the impression you might have had chats like this before.

WILL: Yeah, but not with a woman as hot as you.

ME: [blatantly blushing] Well, you certainly are a charmer. As much as I would like to continue our filthy repertoire, I must go.

WILL: OK, sexy. Until next time. You have no idea how sexy you are.

ME: Thanks, see you tomorrow.

WILL: Yes, you will x

I went home feeling both sexy and violated. Why had Will from the sports desk chosen to chat to me like that? What aura had I been giving off to make him think I would be the girl to talk dirty to? It was fun – in fact, it was exhilarating – but as the angel had been reminding me earlier, this was not good behaviour with a married man. But then, as the devil would say, I wasn't in the wrong, he was.

The next day, I made a conscious effort with my outfit for work. No mini-skirts, but just a nice dress and *those* knee-high boots. Looking back now, they were nasty! But Will had made so many comments, I felt compelled to please him. As I was logging onto my computer that morning, an instant message was flashing – from my boss. Oh, fuck, why was he sending me an instant message? He never did... I opened it nervously: 'Great job on the homeless piece for this morning's breakfast show.' Thank God he was just talking about my follow-up to the previous day's story. As I replied, I could see Will was typing a message.

    WILL: Morning, gorgeous. How was your evening?
    ME: Good thanks, how about you?
    WILL: Yeah, it was fine, just bathed the kids and read
            them a story.

This was lovely and innocent and also made me fancy him even more as he was clearly a great dad, but what was he doing messaging me filth all day?

    ME: How nice! I used to love my dad reading to me
            when I was a little girl.
    WILL: I would like to do more to you than read you a
            story at bedtime.
    ME: What might that be?
    WILL: I would start by kissing you deeply.
    ME: [feeling fireworks of excitement in the pit of
            my stomach] I would like that.

Textual Intercourse

WILL: I would then kiss your neck and around your ears. Then I would move my way down your body, and swivel my tongue around your nipples.

ME: I think they're hard now, just thinking about that.

WILL: What do you like?

ME: To turn you on. I don't think you get better than kissing a man's body, teasing your way down to his rock-solid cock and seeing the excitement/anticipation in his eyes.

WILL: Well, you're doing a good job of getting this big cock 'rock-solid' right now.

At that precise moment Steve, also from the sports desk, walked over to Will and started laughing with him about something. I was terrified it had been about my message.

ME: Please don't tell me Steve saw that message?

WILL: Don't worry, I'm not that fucking silly. Our chat was hidden on the screen. I can't get up right now though, thanks to your horny message.

ME: I can't deny I would like to feel that hard cock, in my mouth and in my...

WILL: Hand?!

ME: I think you know!

WILL: Are you saying you would like my rock-solid cock in your pussy, miss?

ME: I may have implied this.

WILL: Before I do that, I would like to return the favour by running my tongue along your pussy and around your clit.

ME: Will!!! This is too much!

He really was making me distracted. I was supposed to be getting ready for the morning news meeting, arming myself with strong story suggestions. Instead all I could think about was Will from the sports desk running his tongue around my lady parts!

WILL: Are you bottling it?

ME: Yes. This not OK chat, at 10.10 a.m., in a newsroom environment!

WILL: OK, good point. Great fun though, right?

ME: Maybe, but I still feel guilty. You are a married man.

WILL   But we aren't actually doing anything. It's just chat. Have you ever considered we meet and just masturbate in front of each other? The rule is absolutely no touching.

ME: Does that make it OK? The fact we just watch each other but don't touch?

WILL: Yep, we get to turn each other on, but it's guilt-free.

And this was exactly how Will from the sports desk continued to justify our filthy chats. He soon made me realise I wasn't the only 'victim' of his salacious ways. This went on for months. I was obviously just as much to blame and in hindsight I should never have even entertained the idea. In fact, I would go as far as to say that women like me have a lot to answer for. I was young and naive, but I still should have had a stronger moral compass and recognised that 'textual intercourse' with a married man was not acceptable. I should have turned down his advances from the word go.

I honestly think I have become less trusting of men through being the kind of hussy I myself hate. I don't have any justification, other than it was 'banter' and I didn't ever act upon our words. Also, I reckon he would have been one of those men who are more exciting in fantasy than in reality. It was easy for him to talk about 'my big cock' as part of hypothetical sex when I was never going to know the truth. He might have had a chipolata of a cock! And some of the language he used was quite frankly ridiculous. 'Swivel my tongue around your nipples' – I mean, come on, buddy! I'm sure some of the phrases were an amalgamation of sexual terminology and football commentary: 'I want to ram my cock from the corner and straight into your box.'

It was all good fun at the time and there was an extra buzz due to the threat of being caught at work and the risk of us losing it all (both our jobs and his marriage). But it was also not good for me. He was a man I never actually touched and yet he has still impacted me. That sort of misdemeanour has contributed to me being the way I am today, often looking at married men and wondering how many of them are doing exactly the same as Will with a woman like me in their office. All because it is so easy in the digital landscape we live in. Whether it's the instant messaging system at work or email, or more likely Snapchat or WhatsApp these days. All textual intercourse is not OK if one of those taking part is married!

Will never actually committed infidelity with me, but he was still getting kicks from fantasising about it. Surely, when you marry someone and make your vows – for better, for worse, for richer, for poorer, in sickness and in health, to love and to cherish – you could also add, 'Thou shalt not tell another woman how much you would like to taste her.' I cannot legislate for this, but I can say with my hand on my heart that I hope the man I end up with not only physically keeps his cock in his pants, but also his mind out of the gutter when it comes to talking to other women, particularly work colleagues.

ARTIST: Justin Timberlake
TITLE: 'Cry Me a River'
REASON: This song was synonymous with the time I worked with Will. Plus, it was said to be inspired by Justin's break-up with Britney Spears, with rumours suggesting she had cheated on him – his video even features a blonde Britney lookalike.

Chapter 32

Let Sleeping Dogs Lie

I was going to call this chapter 'Haunting the Ghosters' but I had a change of heart.

During my man detox I have been thinking about the sheer number of men who have been in my inbox this year alone. I don't just mean physically (!) but those men I have merely engaged with online and chatted to. Even though my online dating profile says NONS (No One Night Stands), not everyone respects that. Much of the time it has been pretty easy to tell who was after just one thing but on occasion I've got it wrong – meaning, I have failed to spot the warning signs that a man will effectively groom me, woo me, fuck me and fuck off.

Philip was one example. I matched with him on Bumble and I was quick to say that I was looking for a relationship and not a one-night stand. I also told him I didn't like too much messaging and would rather arrange a drink and meet early doors. Philip was very average looking in his pictures. He was a grey-haired accountant from west London, of slim build with lovely blue eyes and clichéd 'I like being active' photos of him climbing and cycling. He was very normal with his messages: 'What do I like? In no particular order: running, climbing, biking, wine, opera, theatre, wine, hiking, good movies on the sofa (preferably with someone else and wine), cooking, cleaning (don't ask!). And did I mention good wine? How about you?'

We exchanged numbers and I discovered that we had actually matched eighteen months earlier. I realised what had happened when the previous round of messages between us popped up when I went to WhatsApp him – both the advantage and the curse of digital communication. When I mentioned this, he said, 'Oh, yes, you ghosted me.' I had completely forgotten about this, and him for that matter. But it gave him some reason to rib me.

PHILIP: So, I think you may owe me one after you ghosted me?!

ME: Well, it depends what you mean by owe you one!

PHILIP: You could start off with a massage...

ME: Oh could I?!

He soon became more flirty and suggestive in his talk about massages. 'I would like to lick all the way up your spine and gently bite the back of your neck, and your shoulders. I'll then lick back down your spine and instead of stopping at the top of your arse, I may just continue down between your cheeks. Would that breach the boundaries of a professional massage? Because there's a good chance that's what I'd do if your naked back was in front of me.'

This was all before we met.

He would also phone me in his lunch hours and update me on the mundane day-to-day, convincing me he was just 'normal'. After chit-chatting for a couple of weeks (too long) we went bowling for our first date. He revealed that he had chosen the activity so he could spend the night admiring me when I bent over, when he could 'check out your arse'. I went along with it and fortunately I managed three strikes, meaning I didn't completely embarrass myself as a novice bowler.

We went for a drink afterwards, but just one as it was a school night. In the lift on the way back to find the car, he grabbed hold of me, pressed me up against the wall and snogged my face off. Although I had been talking to him a lot over the phone and in messages, I didn't really know him that well and so the first kiss felt nice but a bit awkward.

We got in the car and despite being strapped into our respective driver and passenger seats, he started kissing me passionately again, holding the back of my head and gripping my hair. It was nice, but he was *very* keen. He had a young daughter and said he had been in one other relationship since his divorce. I think it had been a while since he had been 'satisfied'.

As we drove, his left hand started creeping onto my leg and under my dress. I don't know how, but while driving his high-powered car, he fingered me all the way home. By the end of the twenty-minute journey I was soaking wet – he certainly knew what he was doing. Slightly flushed, I got out of the car and headed indoors, saying that I'd catch up with him at the weekend. I wanted him to know that I wasn't going to go straight to bed with him, but after we'd got so frisky on the first date, it was hard to go backwards.

We messaged constantly, him sending descriptive messages about what he wanted to do to me on our next date. It was yet another period in which I would always be checking my mobile for the next message (a.k.a. getting a dating junkie 'hit'). His message at 7 a.m. after our first date: 'I have just woken up and can still smell you all over my fingers. Such a turn-on. I couldn't hide how much I want to eat it, the juice was so sweet. I want you sit on my face and let all that juice flood into my mouth. I want to drink you.'

After much textual intercourse, he came over on the Saturday night and we failed to even have any dinner before we ended up going straight in the bedroom. He fulfilled his promises. He was absolutely obsessed with eating me and he was very good at it. Considering his initial safe-looking profile on Bumble he was absolute filth. He wanted to go straight in the 'back door', but I wasn't having any of that. He was clearly experienced and yet he also acted pretty sex-starved. But then his weekends were taken up being a good dad and his work was very demanding, and he was very keen to take advantage of my sexual enthusiasm.

We still went out for dinners and he also cooked for me a few times, but there was an underlying predatory streak to him and an expectation I would satisfy his urges. I went over for dinner one night and in the middle of making fresh pesto and gnocchi, he washed the herbs off his hands and started kissing and fingering me in the kitchen.

It was a boiling hot night and he led me into the bedroom for raw, hard, passionate sex. He had mirrored wardrobes and I could see he was enjoying watching himself ramming me from behind. It was fun, but animalistic rather than romantic.

This went on for a few months until we both happened to be going away for a week on separate holidays. We exchanged a couple of messages, but we had nothing like the intense contact I had been used to. When I got back, I had a couple of messages telling me how busy he was and the last message came from me: 'Let me know when you're free.' Then, nothing. Ultimately, he had groomed me, wooed me, fucked me and fucked off.

As part of this man detox I came up with the idea of Haunting the Ghosters. I wanted to send a message to all the guys who have done this to me. Something along these lines: 'Hey, I got thinking about you the other day and was wondering what happened? We were getting on well, having a nice time/good chats/sex. Was there anything I said/did? Would love to know. Purely so I can learn going forward! Thanks, Vx' After writing the message last night I was tempted to send it straight away as part of the detox. Then I decided to sleep on it – and I'm so glad I did.

This morning I realised a few things. Firstly, sending a message would be breaking my man detox rule of not messaging a man I have slept with. Also, I don't think I did do anything wrong – these men just weren't right for me and vice versa. If they had been right for me, we would still be together. Most of all, I won't lose my self-respect as part of this experiment. They probably wouldn't have replied anyway.

Man Detox

I think it's best to just accept Philip was another dog. A predatory dog. Who wanted to have his cake and most definitely eat it. We had our fun and I didn't get upset about him ghosting me, which tells me a lot. Sometimes it is best to just let sleeping dogs lie.

ARTIST: Florence + The Machine
TITLE: 'Dog Days Are Over'
REASON: Amazing song that is synonymous with my pledge to avoid dogs in the future!

Chapter 33

Humping the Dance Floor

I wonder what the pivotal moments in my lifetime will be? The ones I'll remember when I'm old and grey and thinking back? One of those moments is currently not my wedding, as I haven't had one yet, but my brother's wedding.

It was a rainy Saturday in October, and the first time since their kids had graduated, ten years earlier, that our mum and dad were going to meet. More importantly for me, my younger brother was getting married before me. How excruciatingly embarrassing. I predicted that *all* my uncles and aunties who I would never normally have to see would ask, 'How's your love life, Verity?' They did. Kill me now!

My uncle Gary, for instance, spent my whole childhood asking, 'Where's the boyfriend?' Aged eight, I would reply, 'I don't like boys.' When I was fifteen or so, I would reply to the same question with a more coy, 'I haven't got a boyfriend, but hopefully soon.' And here I was at my brother's wedding, aged thirty-one, with a similar answer.

The wedding was not only full of family I wanted to duck away from, but also all my brother's hot mates. The ones I had always admired but my brother had made clear were out of bounds, as they were *his* mates. He had worked his way through many of my friends over the years, but it was somehow different for his older sister. Maybe I had only imagined it, but it always seemed clear that I wasn't cool or good-looking enough for his mates. But they did know I was good fun, especially after a few too many.

A wedding held somewhere neutral is always fatal, as everyone is on unfamiliar territory and there's an element of 'What goes on tour stays on tour'. This ceremony was held in the grounds of a country house hotel. My brother and his wife-to-be had written their own vows, which were very beautiful and incredibly romantic, but also pretty vomit-worthy. It was lovely, but inside I was insanely sad it wasn't me standing up there in a white dress, exchanging vows in front of our family.

When I think about self-worth, it's often attached to how I have been made to feel by my siblings and how my parents made me feel compared to my siblings. I've always been the bossy big sister who wasn't really as cool as my brother and sister. Maybe this is just in my head, but that's how I felt they saw me at times. Even though I have always been successful career-wise, there haven't been many shining examples in relationships. My brother's wedding was a key moment for hearing a lot of 'You'll be next'-type comments.

One of the most agonising things about going to

weddings when you are alone is being placed on the singles table. I'm sorry, but has *anyone* ever been successful on one of these? Such an excruciating, patronising space in which to dump the unlucky-in-love crew. Then there was my dad trying to play cupid, although he meant it caringly. He tried matchmaking in front of a guy who I had fancied for ages: 'V, how about Mikey B?' I was instantly scarlet with embarrassment. My dad was, after a few too many champagnes, suggesting I should get it on with Mikey B.

Realistically, if it were going to happen between Mikey B and I, it would've happened a long time before now. We had known each other for ages. Mikey was a gardener and handyman who my brother had met while living in London. He was always there on nights out, at birthdays, etc. He was gorgeous, but had never taken any notice of me. He sure as hell was not going to take any notice of me now that my dad had physically shoved us together like Barbie and Ken dolls: 'Come on, you two, you'd make a nice couple.'

Mikey B looked absolutely stunning in the morning suit he wore as one of my brother's ushers. He politely told me I looked nice in my outfit, but I was quick to dismiss his comment. 'I feel like ten-ton-Tessie in this dress, but thanks anyway.' I was wearing a typical wedding dress: blue and frilly, with a netted fascinator. I think my dad thought he and Mikey B were good pals after they had been on the stag do, but being set up by my dad was still an excruciating moment.

The third thing I hate at weddings, or any events of any kind, is organised fun. You are encouraged or forced to dress up in silly wigs and oversized glasses for a photo. Or you have to watch the first dance and then grab your partner to 'join the new Mr and Mrs So-And-So' on the dancefloor. I also hate being told to do a conga, a cèilidh or any of that 'Oops Upside Your Head'-type bollocks. I loathe karaoke or any kind of ice-breaker/team-building games. I guess I had got to the point where I had become a serial guest and I was suffering from wedding fatigue.

Don't get me wrong: my brother's wedding was a great day, but there was a lot of free-flowing booze. I took full advantage of the bar and had a glass permanently in my hand from the start of the champagne reception. As nice as it was, the problem, as ever, with having my glass topped up was being completely unaware of how much I was drinking. And this definitely was not a good idea at my own brother's big day. Due to a late wedding breakfast I was not interested in food by the time it arrived and I reportedly told everyone, 'Eating is cheating.' I remember the early part of the reception, greeting the family and seeing all the uncles, aunties, cousins and friends. Then it got blurry. I was joyfully segueing from one person to the next, discussing what a wonderful day it was, seeing my brother marry the woman of his dreams, to the backdrop of a tinkling pianist.

I think I was also on a mission – a mission to make sure I was not going to end the night alone and without 'love'. There was a great array of people at the wedding who were potential suitors (as my dad kept pointing out). I was also caught in a toe-curling conversation with my auntie Nancy, who talked *at* me about being single, like I was suffering a life-threatening disease. 'Aww, are you *still* on your own, Verity? Have you tried salsa classes? You need to hurry up and meet a nice young man before those eggs dry up.

Humping the Dance Floor

Have you thought about freezing your eggs? My friend's daughter has just done that. I think it's a very sensible idea. You young women these days get so caught up with climbing the career ladder, you forget about that biological clock – tick, tock, tick, tock.' Before I had a chance to interject with a response to her ridiculous idea about salsa classes – which would only be full of women and gay men – she continued, 'Maybe you should think about a sperm donor? That gay housemate of yours, what's he called, he might let you have his child?'

I was completely flabbergasted by the whole conversation. I came back with the quickest, bluntest retort I could think of: 'Auntie Nancy, just because I'm single doesn't mean I don't have sex.'

I left her choking on her champagne after my life-affirming comeback, allowing her to think about the revelation I was a sexual deviant. Fortunately, I caught the eye of one of my best friends and moved on.

I toured around the increasingly spinning room and repeatedly passed a security guard who was busy doing his job, but gave me a wink whenever we saw each other. He was very chatty and wanted to make sure I was having a good time, as I boastfully told him it was '*my* bruutherrr getting married... my baby bruuutherrr.' He helped me up as I tripped up on my own feet to get to the loo. When I came out with lipstick halfway down my face and hair arranged in a worse state than it had been before, I took it upon myself to take the hand of the security guard and drag him through a door marked 'Private'. I whispered to him my classic drunken line, 'We're here for a good time, not a long time.'

Through the private door was a tiny room filled with rows of coats and a stuffed deer's head that frightened the life out of me. The tall, slim, smart-looking security guard laughed at me. 'Why have you brought me in here?' At this moment I grabbed hold of him and started passionately (drunkenly) kissing him. He didn't stop me, but did say, 'I'm meant to be doing my job.' I just assured him that he was doing his job by looking after me. As we continued to kiss, he whispered, 'You know, I've been looking at you all day.'

I knew he had but said, 'Oh, I hadn't noticed.' He smelt very strongly of cigarettes, but something carnal inside me ignored anything unpleasant and continued to let him ravage me with his tongue. He pushed my hand onto his already-firm cock and encouraged me to rub him. I knew even in my fuzzy-headed state what I was doing was wrong, but carried on regardless. It was as if I wanted to prove to myself that, although it wasn't my wedding day, I could still have fun, even it was with a complete stranger who happened to be a security guard. Very quickly we were in a position where we were standing, but leaning on the coats, snogging and me wanking him furiously. There was an explosion of jizz on my hand, down my arm and on a few of the coats. It was a complete mess.

Somewhere in my drunken haze, I had a moment in which I alarmed myself thinking, I don't even know this guy's name! We continued to slobber over each other and he said, 'You're very good at that. Let me return the favour.' But even as far gone as I was, I knew I didn't want any favours returned. I said, 'No, thanks' and that I needed to get back to the party. I knew I was better than this, yet there I was, at my brother's wedding, in a coat closet, with a security guard's jizz all over my hand, down my arm and on my dress. What the hell was I doing?!

I divulge this vulgar story not only as a means of confession – to ask the universe for forgiveness – but also to work out for myself why I did what I did. There was definitely an element of feeling that I had failed as a daughter and as an older sister by not getting married first. I also felt a deep-rooted sadness that I was still single and nowhere near marriage.

I wiped the jizz off myself (with someone else's coat) and came out of the small room, telling Dwayne (I noticed his name badge when we got back in the light) I would see him later. I knew I wouldn't see him later if I could possibly avoid it. I got back into the bustling wedding reception to find my friends on the dancefloor. As there was only eighteen months between my brother and I, we have a lot of the same friends. Knowing what I had just done, I was glad to be back in the cosy embrace of familiar, friendly faces. I went to the loo and tried to patch up my panda eyes and smeared lipstick, but it must have been pretty obvious what I had been up to.

As the evening went on, I continued touring around the dancefloor, drinking and dancing with (grinding against) any man who would let me. I was aware of what I was doing, but the alcohol allowed me to continue. I don't remember getting to bed, but fortunately I only had to get to a room in a barn attached to the hotel. I was sharing it with my sister who was nineteen and impressionable.

My next memory is of being violently sick the next morning, my sister holding my hair back. After I finally managed to sort myself out by drinking plenty of water and having a shower, I was confronted by a very disappointed mother. 'What on earth were you playing at last night?' I just apologised and said I hadn't really eaten much and that was why I had got out of control. 'You were an absolute disgrace, acting like a rampant dog on the dancefloor, humping every man's leg you came across.' She slapped me around the face. Not hard, but it was enough to make the point that I had been a nightmare. Tears starting streaming down my face as I tried to defend myself again and she continued to shout me down. 'How could you be so embarrassing at your own brother's wedding?'

My sister interjected, 'Yeah, V, you were the person everyone tried to avoid.'

Oh God, this remonstration was not helping my thumping head and the irony of it all was that they didn't know the half of it.

I held my head in my hands throughout breakfast and for most of the day. Many wedding guests – including Mikey B – came up to me to say, '*You* looked like you were having a good time last night' – basically the polite way of saying 'You looked a fucking mess.'

Yet I was pleased to see so many of the family again, this time sober. I was still bombarded with 'Maybe it'll be you next time, V,' meaning that we might not see each other again until my wedding. As it turned out, we would see each other at more than one funeral rather than any wedding of mine.

I thought I had gotten away with the whole cloakroom debacle until I came face-to-face with the dubious, crusty white stains that decorated Auntie Nancy's black fur coat.

She was busy getting Uncle Harry to help her brush it off. I knew exactly what it was, but was never going to volunteer the information: 'Oh, that's Dwayne the security guard's jizz on your coat, sorry about that.' Anyway, I couldn't help but feel it was a tiny bit of comeuppance (cum-uppance!) for her 'dried-up-eggs/sperm donor' chat.

The wedding had been incredible, from the vows to the food and drinks to the party and the venue. I wish I could have been in a better headspace to enjoy it, instead of inadvertently going on a mission to 'score' myself a man who was not in any way a potential boyfriend. Maybe Auntie Nancy's attack on my singledom was playing on my mind and I had set out to prove something to myself. It was one of the most disposable, soulless and unsatisfying sexual encounters of my life and all because I wanted someone rather than no one. Fortunately, no one ever found out, but as I piece together why I am where I am at, it's interesting to reflect on these seedy encounters.

I realise I have engaged in so many fruitless acts as a means of finding self-worth, but ultimately I make myself feel worthless. I am really not proud of the occasion of my brother's wedding and it's taken some time for me to clarify exactly what happened that night, but I know none of it was worth it and I can safely say I know I am worth more.

ARTIST: Beverley Knight
TITLE: 'Greatest Day'
REASON: Despite my misdemeanours, it really was the greatest day!

Chapter 34

Childhood Sweetheart

Oh jeez! It's day thirty-three of the man detox and I have had the wonderful, yet gut-wrenching, news that two of my best friends are expecting their *third* babies!

I guess this is to be expected, aged thirty-nine, but this does make me feel completely left on the shelf. Each of these friends married men they'd met at university, effectively their childhood sweethearts. Maybe that's where I went wrong? Should I have seized my first true love and held onto him tight?

I met my first long-term boyfriend on my gap year. He was doing the same job as me, working in a school in Australia, teaching Aboriginal school-kids. It was my first chance to leave home and jet off to see the world. I thought I was ready for it, but when it came to the day, I hadn't really packed, I didn't have any money and I bawled my eyes out at the airport when I waved goodbye to my family. Fortunately, my trip had been organised through a company

261

and everything was laid out for me. There were four of us, David, Harry, Jane and me, doing the same thing, so we got in touch with each other in advance and arranged to fly out on the same plane. Twenty-four hours on the same flight was a good introduction and we immediately gelled. At the time we thought we were so grown-up, each of us eighteen, without a care in the world, going to take on the roles of boarding house parents to dozens of complicated Aboriginal kids.

David was immediately my favourite of the two boys. He was cheeky, with gorgeous blue eyes and a bit of an attitude, whereas Harry was a typical public schoolboy, with floppy hair and a very posh accent. He was a giant teddy bear by comparison with David. David was out to impress from the outset, talking about his love for garage music and clubbing back in the UK. Not something I had ever really been into but I have always enjoyed being introduced to new music and feeding off the passion of someone else's taste. As soon as we got to Darwin, we were quick to explore the local area and find the best bars and hangouts, including the surf club, where we could go swimming in the sweltering heat. It wasn't long before we were on a night out and David and I showed our mutual appreciation with a kiss. He was quick to tell me how experienced he was with girls and this encouraged me to make similar boasts. However, the honest truth was that I was in completely new, childhood-sweetheart, love-struck territory. I couldn't wait to see him every day and the naughtiness of having a romance with a fellow member of staff at the school was such a thrill.

We took a lot of trips away that enabled all of us to bond.

Childhood Sweetheart

It soon became apparent that there was a thing between David and I, but he was very keen to keep it low-profile, as we were working in a Catholic boarding school where 'relations' out of wedlock were strictly forbidden. I am not Catholic, but I secured the position on the grounds I had attended a Catholic school, so I knew how to behave.

The problem was, I didn't know how to behave in the early stages of a new romance with a boy I was completely infatuated with. There was a part of me that felt not good enough to be known as his girlfriend, but with hindsight I should have spent those early stages feeling carefree without worrying about the relationship status. The fact David wanted us to act like nothing was going on between us, even in front of Harry and Jane, made me feel pretty crap. And so my desperation for his attention began.

We started seeing each other that September. We would meet in the dark in the botanical gardens that separated the girls' and the boys' boarding houses. It was full of exotic Australian creatures and we would often be exploring each other's bodies in front of a Huntsman spider or a snake. We had an ongoing joke about whether I was feeling David's python or a real one.

It was thrilling and new and dangerous. As we couldn't go in each other's dorms, we would meet on the beach or at the surf club and play with each other in the sea or even in the swimming pool. There was one occasion when we forgot how susceptible to bites we both were and after a raunchy night on the beach, blamed sand-burn for our sore bottoms, but the cause was in fact sandfly bites! It was so painful and made me resent the fact we could only get to know each other in the 'outdoor bedroom'.

Man Detox

By the time of the Australian school summer holidays in December, we had messed about a lot, but we hadn't actually had sex and were keen to get more time to ourselves. We had booked a youth hostel with Jane and Harry, but decided to take one night in a hotel in Sydney with just the two of us. I can remember it as if it were yesterday, it was so nerve-racking. Neither of us wanted to admit to the other that we were both nineteen and about to lose our V-plates. There were blue, towelling bedsheets on the low-budget hotel bed and it was boiling hot due to a lack of air-conditioning. We were used to the heat after being in Darwin during the rainy season, but this was absolutely sweltering. Fortunately, due to the 'dangerous liaisons' we'd had to engage in, we were fairly at ease with each other and the sex came pretty naturally. The moment when David 'broke the seal' was a bit uncomfortable, but nowhere near as bad as the bloodcurdling descriptions I'd had from some girls. It was the most exciting moment of my life so far.

Afterwards we walked down to Darling Harbour, holding hands, almost walking on air with elation that we had finally done the deed. It wasn't until later in our relationship that he actually made me orgasm through sex, but we were both getting to know each other and ourselves in the new, sexual sphere. I had been so used to him turning me on with his fingers, I had become almost reliant on that. There was no doubt in my mind that by actually having proper sexual intercourse we had bonded on a different level. I'm sure this is the case for most women, that the act of sex is so intimate (particularly the first time) that there is immediately a deeper connection between you and that other person, quite literally. But despite us enjoying being a proper couple when we were alone, David was quick to dismiss me as his mate when we were back in front of the rest of the group. Harry and Jane knew exactly what was going on, but David was insistent that we keep it quiet as we had a responsibility not to have an open relationship while working at the school.

The secrecy made it all the more exciting when we were together. We explored the whole of the east coast of Australia over the course of ten weeks on Greyhound coaches, which was incredible. We saw everything: the iconic Sydney Harbour, the Blue Mountains, the beaches of the Gold Coast and the Sunshine Coast, Fraser Island and the Whitsunday Islands, up to Cairns and eventually across to Darwin. It was an epic trip and, having to spend many hours on buses, David and I would regularly be under a sleeping bag pleasing each other. I would try to mask my enjoyment from his fingertips by listening to my CD Walkman. David would regularly spunk all over the sleeping bag, leaving one of us with a wet patch to sleep on at the next youth hostel. It was filthy and juvenile, but so much fun. Yet I was still battling with the fact he would not kiss me or hold me in front of the others.

There was a bizarre moment when we got to Noosa on the Sunshine Coast, when we'd all had a few too many VBs (Victoria Bitter) and the last thing I ever expected to happen, happened. David was in the shower and I was left in the room with Harry. He was like a gorgeous, slobbery, giant dog – always up for cuddles and ready to laugh at all of my jokes. Without any warning, he came up to me and started kissing me. He was showing me a side of Harry I had not seen before. He was passionate, tactile and genuine with his kiss.

'Where did that come from?' I asked.

He said, 'I just felt like kissing you.'

'You know that David and I are together?'

Looking cowardly, Harry said, 'I know, but he doesn't ever admit it, so I assumed you were still available?'

It was so flattering that Harry was even interested in me. By the very nature of there being four of us gap students together, there was a lot of chat about Jane and Harry getting together, but something was not quite clicking.

Harry pulled away from me and apologised. But I had really enjoyed our kiss: 'You've taken me by surprise, but it's nice to kiss you.' So we continued until we heard the shower turn off, as we knew David was on his way back out.

Although we never discussed it again, that was always a special moment for me. It had almost been a sympathy kiss from Harry, as he knew I so desperately wanted David to openly admit we were a couple, but it was as if he was embarrassed to be with me. This was Harry's way of showing me that David should have felt honoured, instead of treating me like his dirty little secret.

The sneaking around in the bushes and at the beaches carried on until May, when David flew back to the UK. I was desperately heartbroken that what happened between us had ended. A few days after he left, there was a phone call at the boarding house. At a time when we relied on payphones and dial-up internet access for any communication from home, this was always so exciting. It was David.

'V, I've made a terrible mistake,' he said. 'I'm completely in love with you and I shouldn't have left without making sure you are my girlfriend.' I had always acted as if I was completely cool with the situation in front of him, but of course I wanted us to be 'official'. I burst into tears and told him I would love to be his girlfriend.

I had bought a round-the-world ticket, so I was taking my time getting back to the UK via New Zealand, the Cook Islands, Fiji, Tahiti and Los Angeles. It was an incredible way to end an incredible gap year. I was also experiencing my first-ever understanding of the true meaning of love. Whoever I met, wherever I went on my travels, I would tell them about my boyfriend back in the UK. I must have acted like the first person to ever fall in love, but it was magical. It was what love should be about. Two people building up a relationship over time, with common interests and ideals. So much so, that I accepted a place on the same course at the same university as David for the September of that year. I can't believe I did that now, but I was so desperately in love with him, I didn't ever want to be apart from him again.

I had told my mum I would be back in the UK a day later than I actually was. David picked me up from the airport and took me back to his, where we had so much sex I was left in cystitis hell for the rest of that week. But it was all part of the honeymoon period we had never had the chance to enjoy as David had taken so long to admit his true feelings for me. We had inadvertently built solid foundations over the nine months that we were in Australia together. It was always a good talking point, being able to tell new friends at university that we had got together on our gap year in Darwin. And despite a few bumps in the road, we stayed together for the three years of university, both studying for a BA in Politics. We didn't live together, but we lived in each other's pockets, ducking out of lectures so we could have long morning sex sessions. Looking back, it was a bit of a waste that we didn't experience any other relationships at university, but at the time we were in love and didn't want anyone else.

My childhood-sweetheart romance came to an abrupt end when we both started our post-grad careers. David joined the police and I went off to do a master's in broadcast journalism. There was suddenly a three-hour journey between us and our lives were going in very different directions. Essentially the relationship was no longer convenient and we went into the classic post-university break-up. This didn't stop me from being absolutely distraught. I *knew* something was not right when David rejected my calls and failed to reply to text messages. He had found a new life in the police force, with other new recruits and he didn't want me any more. I sent him in the region of eighty texts that day – talk about needy! I was experiencing the first taste of proper heartbreak. I can remember the pain physically manifesting itself when I thought about things like never kissing him again, never sleeping with him again, never holding his hand again and the fact he would become someone else's. How was I going to love someone like that ever again? I can even remember the dinner my mum made me to try to make me feel better – chicken casserole and rice. But I was so heartbroken that the casserole made me want to be instantly sick, so I just forced down a few mouthfuls of rice. I even thought that my heartbreak was going to lead to malnutrition.

Over the following weeks and months I started to heal

and was able to discuss with him that we had simply grown apart, both geographically and mentally. We had four happy years together in the end, but we were kids, with everything to live for. He knew I had aspirations to live abroad again and work my way up in the world of journalism. It was never going to work – a police officer and a journalist! Ultimately, I was eager to spread my wings and see what else the world had to offer, but he was far more interested in staying near his parents. And he went on to do exactly what he wanted to do; work his way up through the police force, marry a fellow police officer and have two children.

I do sometimes think, That could have been me. If I had done what some of my friends did, marrying the boyfriend they were with in their early twenties, I too might be announcing my third child today. I had something very special with David, but as soon as we faced adversity we ended it, because I thought there was something better out there. Was I too quick to give it all up? Or was I right to move on and set sail on the dating high seas in my solo boat? There have certainly been a few times when life would have been a lot simpler with my childhood sweetheart by my side.

ARTIST: Extreme
TITLE: 'More Than Words'
REASON: This song always reminds me of David as it was playing in a beach bar in Australia where we had sex on the beach!

Chapter 35

Cherry

As I think about getting back into the weird and wonderful world of dating, I'm trying to bear in mind everything I've learnt from previous experiences and what I have discovered from writing this book. When it comes to where to meet men, the most obvious place these days is obviously online, but I'm going to have to park a lot of my experiences as bad luck, so that I don't go back online feeling cynical about the current culture. I say current, as I don't believe it has always been so frivolous and hope it improves.

I have always been a bit put-off by Tinder. I think it's due to the calibre of men I have met there. This isn't to say it is like that for everyone. I have many friends who have met the love of their life on Tinder. Maybe it's due to the app's nature, which requires little or no effort. You put up some photos and people swipe right ('yes') or left ('no') on your face. You are not obliged or encouraged to write anything about yourself and, unlike Bumble, if you match, either party can start a conversation.

I think Tinder might have been ruined for me by my first-ever date using the app. He was a man called Larry, from Chicago. His profile picture was a lovely, natural shot of him sat on a sofa with his legs stretched out and a dog on his lap. I lived in LA when I was thirty-five and had absolutely loved the USA. I was keen to live there again, so the fact he was originally from Chicago ticked a box. He also looked quite tall, even sitting down, and he was quite geek chic in his glasses. My opening line was about the 'gorgeous dog' and (of course) his response was, 'The owner isn't bad either.'

He was immediately flirty, talking about how he'd like to cook and take me out. We soon discovered we were both newbies on Tinder. Larry was quick to say, 'Does that mean I'm going to pop your Tinder cherry?' This was accompanied by several cherry emojis and from then on that emoji stuck as a replacement for my name. He claimed he'd been in a long-term relationship and was new to the dating scene after a long time 'chained down'.

Over the following six weeks we messaged morning, noon and night. We went back and forth about each other's daily routines and had general chit-chat. This provided a great insight into our worlds and I felt like I was really getting to know him. It was my first experience of a dating app and it felt really exciting. I had a natural naivety that came with being new to dating app territory, as I applied the same rules I would in the 'outside' world. I had an automatic trust that the person I matched with was genuine, mature and a gentleman. When he asked me if I'd like to go for a drink, it seemed like the obvious next step.

We met at a fairly salubrious venue in Oxford Circus, with lovely cocktails and dim lighting. It was stylish, but not too stuffy. I made an effort by wearing a slinky black dress and Christian Louboutin heels. It wasn't hot, but I had a sweaty top lip and my heart was racing. What was I doing?! I had to get a lift to the top floor of the building to get to the bar and as soon as I stepped out of the lift I heard a voice shout '*Cherrry*!' A man vaguely resembling Larry, as wide as he was tall, came bounding over to me and this loud, brash American flung his arms around me. Oh, God.

ME: Hello, you must be Larry!
LARRY: Cherrry! Come here, let me give you a proper hug.
ME: Sure.

He grabbed hold of me so tightly, I felt like I was a rag doll he'd picked up off the floor. I know we had been talking for six weeks but it still felt overfamiliar for a first meet.

ME: Shall we grab a drink?
LARRY: Yeah, sure, I've already had a couple actually. So I have a tab open. What would you like?
ME: A gin and tonic would be lovely.
LARRY: So, how are you feeling now you've popped your Tinder cherry?
ME: Err, good, I suppose. [giggling nervously]
LARRY: Am I what you were expecting?
ME: [thinking, no, you're much shorter and more

boisterous that I imagined] Yes, you look just like your pictures.

LARRY: You are much better than your pictures actually. I like meat with my gravy.

ME: Err, thanks, I think.

He went to pick up a clipboard on the bar. I thought it was a bar menu at first, but it turned out to be a checklist! This man had brazenly brought a clipboard with a list of features he was looking for in a woman. Hair colour, eye colour and size (with a choice of petite, medium, large or oversized)! There was also a selection of personality traits – e.g. shy, outgoing, bossy, moody. I couldn't believe it. He started to mark off his list.

ME: What are you doing?

LARRY: Oh, I just like to make sure my women fit certain criteria.

ME: Wow! OK, that's weird.

LARRY: Why is it weird? [slightly irked]

ME: I just didn't realise I need to match up to expectations like this on a first date. [thinking this must be a Tinder thing]

LARRY: [puts down clipboard and puts hands around my waist] So, can I ask ...

ME: Yes...

LARRY: OK, I'm gonna put it out there. I like a lotta sex, do you like a lotta sex?

ME: Err, yes... [thinking, Not with you]

LARRY: When did you last have sex?

ME: Err, do you really want to know?

LARRY: Yeah, I'm not really, ya know, feeling it from you right now, Verity. [tightening grip around my waist] So, come on, when did you last have sex?

ME: Err... this morning [looking cowardly]

LARRY: [Almost shoving me aside] What?! You only had sex this morning? Why are you here then?

ME: Because he was not anyone I want to be with long-term.

LARRY: OK, so why are you here?

ME: I've really enjoyed chatting to you online and I thought it would be nice to meet you to see if we have a connection in person.

LARRY: [goes back to clipboard] Well, the fact you've only just had sex *this morning* [shouting] must mean you're not that serious about meeting someone!

ME: Maybe I shouldn't have been so honest.

LARRY: Well, here's the deal... I like to give my women a key, so they are there waiting for me when I get home. How do you feel about that?

ME: Not super-happy, to be honest. Who *are* 'your women'?

LARRY: I just like to make sure my girlfriends are made to feel welcome with their own key to my place. And that way, you can get home, freshen and be ready for me.

ME: I think you and I are looking for very different things. [putting jacket on]

LARRY: OK, but it's your loss. I find it's a very good arrangement.

ME: Can we get the bill, please?

LARRY: Oh, don't be like that. I really want to get to know you.

ME: No way! I'm not going to be part of this, I'm afraid. Good luck finding your swinging partner.

The bill arrived and it was seventy-five pounds. He had clearly had a few drinks before I arrived.

LARRY: You OK to split it?

ME: Err, not really, but OK. [feeling guilty I had screwed up this date with my confession]

LARRY: You're a good girl really.

ME: [muttering] Patronising twat. I'm going to go now.

LARRY: Yeah, it's probably for the best.

I paid my half of the bill with little conversation and could not get in the lift and out of the bar fast enough. The whole experience had been heartrending. Firstly, I had been so hopeful seeing that he looked normal and nice in his pictures. In fact he was shorter and wider than he had portrayed. He wasn't a complete horror show, but he had definitely misrepresented himself in his photos. He was sweet in his conversation online, asking about my friends and family etc., and had given me no indication he was going to turn up with a checklist for candidates for the position of his sex slave! He was a gross little twerp and I deleted him from my Tinder profile as soon as I got in the lift.

I have to be brutally honest with myself here too. I was obviously not in the right headspace to be meeting a new date as I had only just seen James that morning. But I had never counted James as someone I would be in a serious relationship with and it seemed irrelevant. I shouldn't have been so honest with Larry, but I was thrown off-guard by the clipboard and questionnaire. There are a few other hard lessons to be learnt from writing about this toxic encounter.

I don't think I could have done anything differently with the messages, while I was getting to know Larry. However, I should have met him much sooner. Six weeks was a long time to be chatting to someone who wasn't being honest. I also should have stood up for myself when he started getting so nosy about my private life. I should have taken him to task over the clipboard and questionnaire: who *does* that?! God knows what the people in the bar around us must have thought.

I know from my friends Hannah and Graham that you can meet normal, nice people on Tinder and live happily ever after, as they have done. I sometimes wonder if it's a London thing, where the pool of men is so big that it's sometimes more difficult to filter out the dating dross.

Coming across a Larry is not necessarily anything to do with dating apps or websites themselves. I just think it comes back to being better at spotting warning signs and having a quick escape route. From the minute I met Larry, I didn't like him. He was loud, brash, embarrassing and I felt patronised when he shouted out 'Cherrry!' across the bar. But I wanted to give him the benefit of the doubt and hoped it was just a friendly welcome. But as you can imagine, I'm not a big fan of glacé cherries as a result!

ARTIST: Jermaine Stewart
TITLE: 'We Don't Have to Take Our Clothes Off'
REASON: The lyrics are so accurate for this story, and there's that famous line about cherry wine!

Chapter 36

Boomerangs

After spending time reflecting on the rich tapestry of my romantic history, I'm starting to come up with new rules to follow when I go back into the big wide world of dating. One of them will be to avoid 'repeat offenders'. There have been a number of men who have messed me around repeatedly, but was this my fault for letting them back in?

This time last year, I was feeling fairly morose about yet another 'single' Christmas. Everywhere I looked there were adverts for 'gifts for the one you love'. I felt like the only woman on Earth without a partner at Christmas parties (pulling a cracker with myself) and dancing with the gawkiest bloke in the office, instead of feeling the warm embrace of my man. I remember that stomach-churning moment as I watched my sister-in-law open her stack of presents from my brother. As lovely as my family is, it was pretty hard being grateful for a rape alarm from my mother (yes, that really happened) and some smellies (again) from my sister. I can't help but long for the day that I'm passed a little turquoise Tiffany box with my name on it at Christmas from the man I love. But whoever that turns out to be, it's not going to be *this* one...

It was the end of January 2017, that grisly part of the year after Christmas when no one has any money and we're all grateful Dry January is over. I had gone to my friend's birthday drinks, in a pub with a crowd of us sat around a table drinking red wine, eating bowls of chips and having great chat. An hour into the party, Johnny and Neil turned up. They were a couple of guys the birthday girl had met on New Year's Day, only a few weeks earlier. I shook hands with both, pecked cheeks and thought little of it. Halfway through the party, a friend said, 'You know that guy Johnny won't take his eyes off you?' I honestly hadn't even noticed. He was not my type – very fair, skinny, blue eyes, heavy smoker with a West Country accent.

I was busy chatting with my girlfriends but throughout the night Johnny would make a point of popping over to interrupt our conversation, pinch our chips, make flirty comments or offer us drinks. He told us that he had recently split from his wife and three kids. They had lived near London and he was back with his parents near Bristol. Tonight he was staying with Neil. He waffled on, trying harder and harder to get my attention, like a dog who keeps bringing its ball over in the hope you'll throw it.

The party eventually petered out. My friend and I were to share a cab and she wanted to leave, but I was in deep conversation with Johnny so she decided to leave us to it. Johnny was very engaging and when I managed to spill red wine down my green top he was quick to come to my aid with some salt and a paper towel. I found this very caring and could see his dad instincts coming into play. He was quick to be tactile, after more red wine, 'brushing past' my hands and arms while gesticulating.

Before we knew it, the bell for last orders was being rung and Johnny lent in to kiss me saying, 'I guess I should kiss you goodnight.' (Yes, we were that couple drunkenly snogging at the end of the bar, hate them!) He was a great kisser, very commanding with his hands, touching my spine like he was tinkling the ivories. The startling moment when the bar lights came on at closing time, rudely disturbed our passionate kissing. Johnny said, 'It seems a shame to end things here.' We decided it was a good idea that he 'got me home safely'.

We hopped in a cab, snogging and feeling each other's bodies, mainly through our clothes, all the way home. We were pretty outrageous, considering the cab driver could see everything in his rearview mirror. I just didn't care, having had too much red wine. Johnny was very sweet with it, telling me how crazy this behaviour was for a man like him, who had been in a twenty-year marriage. I could tell this was really exciting for him, but it was for me too. We got back to mine and had very drunken sex, knocking over a lamp and making a lot of noise (poor neighbours).

When we woke up the next day our clothes were still strewn across the flat where we'd strip-teased each other into the bedroom, condom wrappers lay on the floor (phew) and my head was *pounding*. My saying is, 'Women and wine are never fine' as I cannot handle mine, especially red. We had a morning-glory fumble and it was nice to 'make love' (as he kept saying) when I was *compos mentis.*

He was very attentive in bed, but he had suffered a serious back injury so we had to be careful not to be too vigorous. He got up and made me breakfast (muesli with chopped banana and toast). It was so sweet of him, finding his way around my kitchen and again, he showed me his instinct to look after me. In my experience this comes naturally to guys who are daddies or who have been in long-term relationships.

We had a lazy morning that turned into going for lunch, with Johnny holding my hand along the street and across the table in the restaurant. He smacked my bum as we walked back to the car: 'You're so my type, you are, I like a woman with meat on the bones.' Charming!

That wasn't the only thing he said that raised a red flag. For example, he'd already decided he was taking me on holiday later in the year and even discussed us moving in together. What?! I'd only met him twelve hours previously! These elaborate gestures continued until we parted, when he told me he was heading back to the West Country that night, but would be back by the weekend to take me out.

We had regular phone calls and messages that week. He was super-keen, until 'something came up'. I think he'd freaked himself out with his own empty promises to whisk me away and treat me. I was cynically going along with all of it, but in my heart of hearts didn't really believe him. What I didn't expect was the outright ghosting. Instead of making his excuses, he completely vanished. I asked the friend who had introduced us if this was normal behaviour for him and after a bit of digging, she found out from Neil, 'Johnny's got a really shit phone, but don't worry, he really likes you.' Weeks passed and I just put him down as another great Houdini.

I moved on, buried the whole saga and put him in the 'his loss' pile of toe-rags. By December, I was dreading another oh-so-single Christmas when, completely out of the blue, Johnny tweeted me. Yes, tweeted me. I was so embarrassed for the world to see the public message, 'Hey V, hope you're well? Must catch up soon.' He acted like we were long-lost friends who should be meeting up. I had heard via our mutual friends he had been having a tough time with his divorce and getting custody of his kids, so I decided to be the bigger person and reply (via a private message). He gave me his new mobile number and when I texted, he called me immediately.

He told me everything that had been happening in his life throughout the year. All of the rumours about his complicated divorce were confirmed and he said he had been in a 'bad place' mentally. After an hour-long chat, he asked if he could take me out for dinner to 'make it up to me' for disappearing. Enough time had passed that I was able to forgive and forget about him dropping me from a great height. We met for dinner in a lovely country pub and sat by the fire, catching up. It was Christmas, the pub was dimly lit with pretty fairy lights and we huddled in a corner in a big squidgy sofa where no one could see us. He kept asking, 'What is a gorgeous woman like you still doing single?' I quipped that I was 'constantly being ghosted by men who promised me the Earth'.

At the end of the night he took me back to the farmhouse belonging to his parents where he was living after the financial ruin of his divorce. He really wanted me to meet his parents and have a Christmas drink with them. They had already gone to a church carol concert by the time we got back, so he showed me round the house. It was a beautiful home, with family, school and university photos. We ended up in a cosy lounge where we started kissing.

It was really nice to kiss him again, despite his bad behaviour. I told him I needed to get home, so we made an arrangement for me to pop over the next day to meet his parents and have a coffee and a mince pie. I wasn't really sure why he was so insistent on me meeting them, but he just said that he had told them about me, as I was the only person he had slept with since he'd split up with his wife.

He came to pick me up at 9.30 a.m. He screeched to a halt in his Range Rover outside the house and tooted, ensuring all the neighbours were drawn to their curtains. When we got back to the farmhouse, I was greeted by a bouncing labrador. 'Don't mind her,' Johnny said, 'she's just my sister's guide dog.' I walked into complete madness in the kitchen.

The parents were lovely, but threw their arms around me as if I'd known them all my life. The sister was also lovely, but being blind insisted on feeling every part of me as she met me. A bit like being patted down at airport security. It was fine, but quite a lot to cope with first thing in the morning from someone I'd never met. The whole thing was bizarre. The family sat down at the kitchen table and offered me mince pies with my coffee. They practically interrogated me about who I was, where I worked, where I lived, why I was single, how many brothers and sisters I had, who my parents were, etc.

When Johnny eventually said he would take me home,

I was so relieved. I endured a very huggy and touchy-feely goodbye from all the family. Johnny and I arranged in the car that he would come and take me out after Christmas. We snogged each other goodbye and continued to chat over messages throughout the following few days. On Christmas Day itself, I didn't hear a thing. Oh God, here we go again, I thought. I understood he would be busy with his family, but thought it was pretty rude to not at least send a 'Happy Christmas' message. Annoyingly, I let this ruin my day.

I was distracted by the joy of Christmas with my family, but it was pretty heartbreaking watching all the couples around me exchange gifts when the man I had invested yet more time and headspace in, couldn't even send me a festive text. Why had I allowed myself to get back on a rollercoaster with a guy who had previously hurt me? It was like self-harming. OK, it's not so physically damaging, but why did I let Johnny back in emotionally to chisel another chunk out of my heart?

My gut instinct was right. I didn't hear from him until the day we were meant to meet up and as before, he said that 'something had come up', this time with some long-lost aunt. Whatever! He was a total shitbag who had messed me about not once but *twice* in one year! To add insult to injury, I heard from our mutual friends a few days later that I was not the only girl he had taken home to meet the parents at Christmas. WTF?! What on earth did his sweet parents and touchy-feely, blind sister make of that? Two women for their Johnny at Christmas!

Almost a year later, I can laugh at it all. But I also feel like I must remember all of the mental torment I went through by being so forgiving and allowing him to be a repeat offender. When I go back into the world of dating, there will be *no* boomerangs!

Chapter 37

Best Version of Me

I think I have spent my entire life looking at other women, wishing I was thinner, prettier, more intelligent, richer, more successful, younger, faster, dressed better, etc. I know I am not alone with this, as I have a number of friends who have been aiming to get in shape or lose a few pounds before they meet a man or make sure they have bought a house before they go on dates.

I wish I could replicate life in Los Angeles, where the sun is always shining and people have more confidence. It's not uncommon to see a Californian girl look at herself in a changing-room mirror and say, 'Oh my God, I look *so* cute!' It's just as common to hear a British woman stand in front of the mirror and say, 'Oh my God, I look so awful.' Us Brits can be self-effacing to the point of self-destruction.

The reason I've decided to tackle this issue in myself is because it's absolutely key to understanding where my head has been at with men. I don't have a deep sense of self-loathing but I have always undersold myself, which in turn has meant a lot of the men I have dated and/or slept with have been tools to boost my confidence, even if my needs go unrequited. It starts from the very beginning on dating apps, as you have to 'sell' yourself in a profile and it's very easy to go down the self-deprecating route.

I decided to do a little exercise, to make sure I come out of this man detox with a better understanding and appreciation of myself. This is so that going forward I will present the best version of me to men. I have been completely honest with how I feel.

I am a thirty-nine-year-old newsreader/radio presenter, who feels old in a young industry, but I still love what I do and enjoy the benefits of having experience. I have been around the block a bit in the romance department, with many fun times but quite a lot of bad luck along the way too. I like a lot of sex and need to meet a man who can keep up. I am impatient, have a short attention span and like to be busy. I have lived all over the world and would like to meet someone who likes to do that too; someone who has the get-up-and-go to work abroad and experience different cultures. I love nice food, but could do with eating less sugar and trimming down the chubby hips and thighs. I'm confident enough to wear a bikini but would like to get back into personal training so I can be the best version of myself. I love the great outdoors, cycling and walking to explore places. I like keeping fit and go to my spinning classes and circuit training as much as possible. I have the most amazing friends and family who are my world. I am Aunty V to my gorgeous nephew and dozens of my friends' children. I have not had children because I have not been in a suitable relationship, but the older I get, the less I know if it will happen, but I hope it does as I think I would make a good mum.

As part of the experiment into how I view myself versus how other people see me, I decided to ask people around me to send me a description of me. I sent a message to a few people who have known me for a long time, along with a couple of colleagues from work. I asked for warts-and-all descriptions! And these were the results of my experiment:

From SB:

Gosh, where do I start in this synopsis of my pal of twenty-eight years?

Her name means truth, very apt as I'm writing the truth and she is truth personified. What you see and hear is what you get: honesty in a blue-eyed package.

But to me there's more to this package than that – there's a whole V-E-R-I-T-Y to discover.

V is for vivacious and that's where it all began for our friendship. Her gutsy, bubbly nature started our relationship when we were ten. She'd just joined my school, wanted to be friends with me, so walked all the way to my house to deliver a packet of pocket money-bought dolly mixture sweets through my letterbox. Sealed the friendship deal for me. V is also for Virgo – she's that by the lorry-load. If you know what Virgos are like (and I'm one too so clearly biased) then they have some very super attributes.

E is for energy – mental energy to achieve her career, and physical energy – she is not afraid of cycling from x to y and would rather be out and about, seeing and doing things than lazing in bed – unless there's a good reason to stay in bed – er, hmm.

R is for rack, yes, she has one, a sizeable one that she has inherited from Mother Nature, not a master silicon surgeon. Take it or leave it – sometimes it's out, sometimes it's hidden – but it is very much part of her and her persona.

I is for independence and she has that by the bucketful: perfectly capable of manning a radio show, changing a tyre (?!), and navigating her way. She is one powerful, strong-minded person.

T is for tidy and travelling – even her bedroom when she was fifteen was a picture of orderliness and travelling is something she has done a lot of and is itching to do more.

There is a strange mixture that so many girls are – of wanting to cuddle someone on the sofa on a Sunday night and yet also travel to new places for months on end – and that is part of the reason for Y...

Y is for why is she single? Well, that's an interesting one. She's been single but dating what turn out to be losers/not-rights for a looong time. Maybe that makes you fussy, maybe she's fussy, who knows! I've heard about all the frogs and their pond antics but definitely not enough about princes.

From SE:

Well, where do I start...

Qualities: honesty, happiness, easygoing, caring, believable, good listener, sensitive and loyal. A positive and happy mist surrounds my Verity.

Visually: beautiful, super-sexy (your super-power) and hot, blonde, those large blue eyes that are a knockout, eyelashes that brush my cheeks when I speak to you, breasts to rest on.

Country girl by birth, not really now, but may shack up with a man again in a few years in a field. Jury's out.

Humour: you are hilarious. Worth highlighting this one. Observant of others and cuts through the bullshit with funny and laugh-out-loud humour.

Career: super-skilled and experienced in broad-casting. Listening to you on the radio always makes me proud. A rare skill and I am not sure you realise how good at it you actually are (men be warned of Verity's abilities).

Friendship: a fantastic, reliable and a best friend. One in a million. To the men out there: you are not worthy of my special Verity.

From RH:

There's not a woman alive who eats more brunch than Verity. She's a very good friend, kind and very good at making the effort. She always makes the effort!

She falls in love on an almost weekly basis. Loves big rugby players and anyone who looks a bit like Idris Elba. She loves food and sometimes eats it in date.

Socially she's very at ease in all environments and can talk to anyone. Occasionally she says stuff that she doesn't realise is a bit on the '70s Alf Garnett scale.

She is always up for a laugh. She's got bags of energy and is always slightly over-dressed. She works very hard and has a great work ethic, she's smart and diligent and very reliable.

She loves a celebrity name-drop!

She's dying to meet Mr Right and have kids and regular brunch dates with her girlfriends. She wants more than she currently has in her life. She wants to live in LA in the future. She's honest.

From HS:

Verity Geere doesn't know how to coast, she doesn't live in a world where she operates in anything other than sixth gear. Verity is always ready for something exciting to happen. This is all the more remarkable when you consider that she wakes up at 4 a.m. every weekday for her double-headed national breakfast show. It's one of the qualities about Verity I admire the most: no matter what may be going on outside of her professional world, she's ready with a smile, a joke or some interesting point. There hasn't been a day that she hasn't made me laugh. I enjoy being in her presence. I feel Verity is a person who could literally make friends with any human being on this planet so long as they understood kindness. They wouldn't even have to speak the same language. There's a lot you can ascertain from a smile and Verity is ready with a welcoming one.

Best Version of Me

It's too easy to simply say, 'I like Verity,' but the truth is, if you asked ninety-nine per cent of the people who know her, they would say the same. She's likeable and that's down to her attitude. I work with numerous different personalities, the media world seems to attract so many varying types that it's impossible to pigeonhole any one of them, but Verity is someone you would meet, spend a bit of time with and think, Yeah, I could survive on a desert island with this person. It would certainly be many months of living off coconuts before I even considered butchering her for sustenance. Some people willingly make the day worse and some brighten up the darkest doldrums. I think you can guess by now which one Verity is.

If I was to describe Verity to a friend of mine who hadn't met her I'd say: funny, self-assured, positive and ready for adventure. My friend would likely (and quite rightly) say that that sounds like a cheesy, pre-rehearsed sentence from a dating profile but I'd ignore them. Now it's true that sometimes it can seem like Verity isn't always paying attention but I've been told by even my closest friends that I have a tendency to ramble, so that may not be entirely her fault!

Finally, I'd say Verity is a person you could trust. Someone who likes things to have their place, respectful of others and knows what she wants.

From LB:
I first met V in 2001 at university whilst studying for an MA degree in broadcast journalism. We've been best friends ever since and I know she is always there

for me and vice versa. She is gorgeous, funny, kind, generous, wears her heart on her sleeve and is just generally one of my favourite people to be around. Despite all these attributes, she attracts the wrong type of men. She has done ever since I've known her. My one wish for V is that she meets someone who loves her as much as all her friends and family do.

From PS:

The first time I met Verity, she outlined a small-business proposition. It would, to be honest, have been a tough sell at her local Barclays. The plan centred on using her vocal talents for something a little more, erm, personal than reading the news.

Was I being invited to invest? Was this a bizarre, late-night version of *Dragon's Den*?

That was more than ten years ago, since when she's chased after celebrities with a microphone, run around Los Angeles with a TV camera, and had her face plastered all over London's bus shelters.

Through all those changes, the instability and the horrendous working hours of a career in broadcasting, she's always been one of the funniest, sharpest people in whatever room she happens to be in, as well as being unerringly kind and caring.

We occasionally – far less often than I'd like – exchange gossip over microwaved porridge at the crack of dawn. Annoyingly, she looks far more glamorous at 6 a.m. than anyone has a right to.

And if she ever revives that bizarre business proposition, I'm in...

Although I sent the same message to everyone. One friend misinterpreted what I meant and just wrote a profile for me...

From DW:

What do I want – I want to meet a man I find attractive and fancy, physically and mentally as well as sense-of-humour-wise.

Maybe in the past I have been too trusting – hopeful that the person would be genuine so perhaps now I am slightly guarded.

You can trust me but please treat me well and respect me.

I am looking for something serious and simply don't want to get into something for fun or a good time.

If things don't work out just be up front – I'm a big girl.

I am very sociable and have a big group of friends, some very close.

I am loyal, fun and caring but beyond this life doesn't have to be serious all the time.

Perhaps for me now is the time to get to the next stage of life and I want to do that with someone special who truly wants the same things.

I have had my fair share of fickle blokes so I know what I don't want.

I don't want any games, regardless of how special you are.

Oh, and I love shagging!

From CA:

What can I tell you about Verity? The first thing you notice is her looks. The pneumatic figure, blonde hair and the biggest, brightest blue eyes you've ever seen turn heads. But there is much, much more to her than this. She likes to talk. A lot. Remember that she is a journalist and therefore is not afraid to ask some probing questions! If you can keep up with her fast-paced conversation and hold her attention, then well done – you have passed stage one!

I met Verity at school, aged fourteen, and she had ambition before most people even knew what that was. She made me laugh more than anyone I had ever met. Proper out-of-control laughter when the tears ran down our faces and we didn't think we could stop. She was like a part of my family. She is emotionally strong: when I met her she was dealing with her parents' divorce and yet she was always there for me when I went through the same thing. She made the worst time of my life much more bearable and I will be forever grateful to her for that. She is also physically strong: I'll never forget her picking up my mum's heavy suitcase and carrying it for miles as if it was nothing.

Verity is always busy. She has imagination and drive. She has travelled all over the world and I have never known her to sit back and wait for life to happen. She is compassionate, generous and hilarious. She is very down-to-earth and doesn't take herself too seriously. She might come across as loud and uber-confident, but those who know her best know that she is the kindest and most gentle soul you could imagine.

I'm not sure why Verity is still single. I know that she has high standards, which is a very good thing. I also know that her childhood experiences of relationships and divorce have affected her deeply, which is a very sad thing. Verity's greatest loves are her family and friends. Now I would like her to meet someone who is worthy of being the other great love in her life.

This might seem like an incredibly self-indulgent act of self-validation, an ego-stroking exercise, but it was such a humbling experiment and almost one I wish I had done before. There is not a huge gulf between the way I view myself versus how my colleagues and friends view me, but it has been a big reminder of the things I need to focus on when I'm meeting a man for the first time on a dating app or in person. Without meaning to, I can use negative words that are self-deprecating. My theory is that like attracts like. If I portray a desperate/insecure image, I'll attract desperate/insecure men.

So I have had another go at writing about myself, now that I have offloaded so much in my man detox and heard what my friends had to say:

I am a happy, bubbly, confident thirty-nine-year-old, with amazing friends and family. I have lived all over the world and want to meet a man who is up for doing that too. Hoping to meet a man who is up for having fun, experiencing new things and has a big heart!

Man Detox

ARTIST: Alicia Keys
TITLE: 'Brand New Me'
REASON: The lyrics are so in sync with how
I am feeling. I'm not who I was before!

Chapter 38

Filters

It's 15 January and after two and a half months on my detox, I've been asked by quite a few friends how long I will continue. I've also been asked if I have enjoyed it and what I have learnt. I haven't decided if there will be an end date, but I already know that having a break from men has made me feel stronger and clearer about what I want and what I don't want!

I have also learnt so much about myself and the current dating climate. My willingness to believe what people say on a dating app has left my fingers burnt a few too many times. We live in such a 'filtered' world, brainwashed into believing everyone's Facebook and Instagram posts are a true reflection of their lives, and it is the same in the dating game. But it's incredibly difficult to sift out who legitimately holds the qualities we desire.

Who is the real person behind that photo or profile? Are they genuinely looking for a relationship? Have they filtered their photos beyond recognition? I am holding my hands up here too, by the way, as I am also prone to posting an overly filtered, pristine version of myself when the reality is I'm crying myself to sleep with palpitations after overthinking everything that is wrong in my life.

I can safely say I don't care if a man has a six-pack or owns a fast car. I am more interested in a man who wants to commit to a loving, loyal relationship. This is hard to convey in a dating app profile, but in the past I have definitely been guilty of swiping right on the flashy types.

I also want to be able to leave that toxic world of feeling insecure about what men 'like' online. This so tricky when a relationship starts on the premise that they have 'liked' your profile. But I know I am not alone in feeling jealous when I have seen my man 'like' or 'love' the posts of other women. Or worse still, I have looked up the photos and posts of their exes, tormenting myself with how they look compared to me. This is toxic behaviour and I need to break free from this.

Having taken the rollercoaster ride of detox, pouring out my heart and digging deep into my soul for answers, I recognise the impact of the various men in my life. I realise I have been letting anyone with a heartbeat come near me. I have gained clarity about who I am and who I want to meet. I have had an epiphany – my love life needs to look like my email, with clearly defined folders and much stricter filters in place. With these clear parameters, I will be able to put much tighter controls on who is allowed anywhere near my fanny (my inbox).

Filters

Post-man detox filters

Inbox: hard-earned position of certified lover
Drafts: men who are working to get the inbox position
Sent: men I have scared off
Junk: men who have been disrespectful and don't
qualify for further dates
Archive: the men who have shaped me, remain a
cherished part of me, but don't need to be contacted
Trash: massive collection of men who needed to be
deleted from my life due to their toxic impact

Now, when potential dates come into my life, with my new-found wisdom I am able to assess where they fit in my dating folders. I also need to up my game with my emotional intelligence and communication. No more using that purple aubergine emoji, which is probably my most used emoji! No more sending dirty photos or videos to potential boyfriends or lifetime partners.

ARTIST: Paloma Faith
TITLE: 'Your Ex'
REASON: Such great lyrics about the toxic side
of social media.

Chapter 39

V for Victory

When I tell friends about my blog and my book, the main question has always been, 'Why?'

To remind you where I was at the beginning of this process of unpicking my dating history and ultimately looking into my dating well-being: I was on my knees. I was crying, I was in physical pain with heartbreak. I didn't know where to turn, so when my friend suggested I 'take a break' from men and dating, I turned to my laptop.

I have always found writing cathartic, but I never imagined that by doing my own, self-imposed man detox I would achieve anything of significance. I didn't think I needed professional therapy, I just knew I needed to do something different. I have been completely honest and I have exposed my vulnerability, initially on my blog and then in this book. This has, hand-on-heart, been one of the best things I have ever done.

I wanted to understand if it was me or the current dating

climate that had left me feeling in such a low place when it came to men. Prising open my own Pandora's box of male misdemeanours, it was no wonder to find I was feeling the way I was! (By the way, I have not written about the whole of my dating history, just the ones I feel have registered on my current heartometer, the barometer of the heart.)

I can confidently say something inside me has switched. I have been able to meet up with men in my life who once caused me heartache and assess them with clear eyes. For example, seeing Simon gave me an epiphany – I don't want a man who wants me as his post-divorce plaything.

I have also had enough time away from Ben and James to recognise that both were doing me more harm than good. At the start of this book James had not been off the scene very long. After nearly eight years of him being my fuck buddy I found the strength to see him and tell him I can't have sex with him any more. He was not very happy about it, saying, 'If we can't have sex then we aren't anything.' This told me everything I needed to know. I had been fooling myself all that time that we were friends as well as sex buddies. However, as I suspected, he is incapable of any kind of relationship with women, unless it is for sex. I know I will *never* sleep with him again and I might never see him again either. I thought I would feel sad about this, but to move forward and maintain my dating well-being I have to steer clear of my toxic past. I recognise that I am more than a booty call. James was not good for me. I had many of my nearest and dearest tell me along the way that I was better than that, but I had to see it for myself. He used me for sex, he never contributed a single penny towards all the lunches I provided and there were a couple of occasions he borrowed money and I never saw it again.

When I look at the incredible friends I have maintained healthy relationships with, I know I would never accept behaviour like that from them. If I felt like I was being trodden all over, kept waiting or even stood up, as James did over and over again, I wouldn't put up with it. For so long I accepted this from him, just for the sake of a meaningless fuck on a Tuesday afternoon. I am thrilled to say James is now in my dating archive, where he will remain.

As for Ben, he is still bobbing around in the background of my friendship group and I have no hard feelings. That ship has sailed. He had his chance to try and fight for me, but he didn't. As much as I fancied him, in the end he was too weak-willed. I need someone who takes action to be with me, not just say it. He is dedicated to his daughter and, for all I know, still in a loving relationship with his supposed ex. After stepping away from the situation during the man detox, I totally understand what all my friends told me all along: 'He's not good enough.'

As with so many situations in life, you have to come to your own conclusions with relationships. I had people telling me until they were blue in the face that both James and Ben were useless.

I am not the only one who is going through this. I have a friend with an ex from years ago who keeps her dangling, promising her elaborate commitment one minute and ignoring her the next. There's another man who just hangs around like a bad smell and she keeps him sweet, as she still thinks he's a potential lifetime partner even though he is only twenty per cent certain he wants kids and she is adamant about being a mum. And then she's got a third man who is in and out of prison and rehab, has got money out of her and treats her like shit! When I say, 'Walk away from all of them, they are no good,' she just says that it's easier said than done. She will need to come to her own conclusions about all that, and I hope she does so soon.

I am not forgetting that I was exactly the same for such a long time. I was joking with friends, 'I've got a few men on the go,' but ultimately I was miserable. I was accepting scraps from an array of men. I also think I had become conditioned to believe that I wasn't going to be happy unless I got married and had children – *fast*! This meant I was even swiping right on men simply because they looked like they might have good genes for making babies, rather than looking for someone who was actually a decent person, who would have my back, and would want to enter into a loving relationship.

Society has changed so much, even in the time I've been an adult. I grew up at school planning the time I would get married, how many children I would have and what their names would be. I was then encouraged to get a degree and have a career, and my aspirations to get married and settle down got sidelined. I really feel like a product of the generation who were told we could have it all. But we also feel divided, between being career-driven and being conditioned to believe that success equates to a career *and* a marriage with kids. Hence, in my late thirties I started to panic that if I didn't have the family unit, I had failed. Maybe I should have listened to the people tapping me on the shoulder in my early thirties who asked me when I was going to settle down. Like Auntie Nancy, who was trying to do me a favour when I was at my brother's wedding, by encouraging me to remember my biological clock.

The thing is, I'm coming to realise that having a family is not a true measure of success or happiness. I saw a tweet the other day that summed it up beautifully: 'Everybody always asks if you have a career, if you're married, if you have children, like life is some kind of grocery list. But no one ever asks us if we are happy.'

I started my man detox completely clueless about whether it would work. But I finally feel the freedom to be me. By laying myself bare in this blog-turned-book, I have had the revelation I needed – to be me and to be seen. I have been repeatedly told that I am brave for doing this, as I have allowed myself to be vulnerable and exposed. Yet, it has been through admitting where I have been going wrong that I have found my own self-worth. I have discovered that talking about sex isn't and shouldn't be forbidden. Sex is life! I am highly sexed; it's part of my biological makeup and personality. That's fine, but I have come to realise that I created a lethal combination when I mixed my enjoyment of sex with using sex to validate myself.

I have a zest for life, which I can express and cherish rather than suppress, because I am good enough. I have no idea what will happen to me next, but as I hurtle towards forty, I am not fearful of being on my own any more. I've even done that clichéd thing of chopping all my hair off! It's so liberating. I am also not scared of loving with my whole heart. I can recognise now that although there's no guarantee love will work out, all the heartbreak I've experienced has made me who I am today. Instead of assuming that every relationship will be a catastrophe from the start, I'm willing to open up my heart and let myself be loved.

I have been blown away with the reaction I have had to my 'waffle', as I have consistently called it. So many men and women have told me they have similar stories of disasters in the bedroom, stories of heartbreak and disposable dating. Some of my older readers have told me they can't believe how complicated the dating world is these days. Many people have asked what I have been doing instead of dating and the simple answer is, concentrating on me! Just doing what I set out to do, which is rid my body of dating toxins, celebrate the good, and work out who I am and what I want.

I would never say that doing a man detox works for everyone, but it has for me. Giving myself the time to take stock, and reflecting on the current digital dating arena, has taught me so much. My biggest epiphany has been discovering that maybe I have always been OK just the way I am. This chapter is called 'V for Victory' because I honestly feel this book is a V-sign to all those men who hurt me and a victory for V (me)! Instead of wishing I was someone/something else, to fit the mould of the men I've met, I've realised that I need to be better at being my true self.

My biggest news is that I have met someone. A man who has actually been on the periphery of my life for three years, but until last year was married and unavailable. He popped up on my Bumble last summer and I ignored it, as I was too scared to swipe right. At a party at Christmas we got talking and admitted that we had seen each other on Bumble, but neither of us thought we would like each other.

We have only been on a handful of dates and are still

getting to know each other, but I feel like I have had an awakening by meeting him. He has also taught me that the very nature of swiping left and right based on gut instinct can be wrong. It's a split-second decision and my reasons for swiping left were wrong. I didn't think he would like me: WRONG. He wasn't available: WRONG. Why would he be on Bumble in the first place? In that moment I decided he must be looking to be unfaithful to his then-wife – which was more to do with where my own head was at the time.

I hate people who say this, but it is so true – partners come along when you least expect it. In my case, he was always there, but I didn't think he would like me. Instead, he has fully embraced everything about me, including the fact I have been writing this book! That's a big ask. He also tells me every day that I am sexy, gorgeous, funny, kind, and have magnificent boobs and bum, etc. He's even given me a Tiffany Infinity necklace, completely unprompted and out of the blue. He had no idea that I'd written about my desire for one in the book.

Most importantly, we have an amazing friendship, something that has been missing with so many of the disastrous men in my life. I had not had strong foundations with other men and many relationships consisted only of me and another stranger leaping into bed together. No wonder they didn't last! Now, we laugh incessantly about stupid stuff, we respect each other and we can't wait to get to know each other more.

This is why I am not sad about the fact that he is moving abroad for eighteen months with work. Yes, pretty bad luck. However, I truly believe that *if* we are meant to pass the test of time, we will. And if we don't, he has still taught me more than any other man ever has, and that is, not to be scared of love.

ARTIST: Rudimental featuring Ray BLK
and Stefflon Don
TITLE: 'Scared of Love'
REASON: We have all been bruised by love but we shouldn't be fearful of it.

Glossary

Breadcrumbing – to string someone along. Blowing hot and cold with attention. Luring in with sexual flattery one minute and disappearing the next.

Bumble – online dating app.

Catfish – a person who creates fake personal profiles on social media sites using someone else's pictures and false biographical information to pretend to be someone other than themselves.

Cock – penis.

DEmenBER – a continuation of *NOmenBER* (cf.) into the month of December.

Fuck buddy; FB – a casual sex partner.

Friend-zone – one partner wants a romantic relationship while the other wants a friendship.

Ghosters – those who groom, woo, fuck and fuck off without a trace.

Handsy – someone you don't know well who likes to liberally rub all over you.

Happn – online dating app.

Heartometer – a barometer of the heart.

Man detox – a period of time when one gives up dating in pursuit of self-discovery.

NOmenBER – giving up men for November, can continue to *DEmenBER* (cf.).

Pussy – vagina

Slumberland test pilots – men who make it their goal to sleep with as many women as possible.

Submarines – men who were once met/dated/fucked and then disappeared without a trace before popping up again when they are feeling lonely/need some attention, as if nothing has happened

Tinder – online dating app.